Foreign Affairs
What Was the Liberal Order?

Foreign Affairs March 2017

The World We May Be Losing

TABLE OF CONTENTS

Introduction

Gideon Rose

The United Nations headquarters, New York.

Don't it always seem to go that you don't know what you've got till it's gone?

The central fact about international politics is anarchy, the lack of a common sovereign authority able to settle disputes and establish order. This has meant that throughout history, states have been forced to fend for themselves, protecting and advancing their national interests as they see fit, embracing whatever policies and temporary partnerships seem expedient.

Life in such a self-help system is precarious. As Thomas Hobbes noted, "Without a common power to keep them all in awe," the players in the game have to worry constantly and make sure the other players aren't trying to screw them. In such circumstances, he observed,

---

... there is no place for industry, because the fruit thereof is uncertain: and consequently no culture of the earth; no navigation, nor use of the commodities that may be imported by sea; no commodious building; no instruments of moving and removing such things as require much force; no knowledge of the face of the earth; no account of time; no arts; no letters; no society; and which is worst of all, continual fear, and danger of violent death; and the life of man, solitary, poor, nasty, brutish, and short.

Over the centuries, this coordination problem has contributed to countless depressions, crises, and wars. Anarchy allows bad leaders and bad regimes to wreak havoc. But it also makes it hard for even not-so-bad regimes to cooperate with one another reliably enough for everyone to stop being so suspicious, relax a bit, and turn their attention to the business of living productively.

In the 1940s, as they suffered through yet another round of destruction and turmoil, policymakers in Washington and other major Western capitals finally decided that enough was enough. They recognized that the horrors of the first half of the twentieth century had emerged because their countries had hunkered down in the face of economic and geopolitical crisis, passing the buck rather than fighting together against their common enemies. So they swore not to repeat their mistakes and designed a postwar order based on mutually beneficial cooperation.

Acknowledging that anarchy would continue to persist, they sought to overcome the coordination problems it posed through sheer strength of will and reason. They chose to see international politics as resembling not Hobbes's state of nature but John Locke's—as a realm in which the players did not simply have to suffer or submit to Leviathan but could follow a third path, voluntarily binding themselves together for common advancement. They linked their countries to one another in international institutions, trade agreements, and military alliances, betting that they would be stronger together. And they were correct: backed by extraordinary and enduring American power, the system they created has flourished, underwriting seven decades of progress, greatpower peace, and economic growth.

Today this liberal international order is a bit dilapidated. The structure still stands, but paint is peeling, walls are cracking, and jerry-built additions jut out from odd angles. Even at its best the arrangements never fully lived up to their ideals, and benefits have not always been distributed equally or fairly. Slowing growth, increasing inequality, declining social mobility, excessive bureaucracy, self-dealing elites, poor responses to transnational problems such as terrorism and climate change—the litany of current problems is long and familiar. And with its great ideological rivals vanquished, the authority of the order must now be judged by actual performance, not simply comparison with even more dysfunctional competitors.

Major renovations are clearly called for, and they will inevitably be slow, difficult, and costly. Still, most of the challenges involved are manageable, and the system has plenty of capacity and resources to deploy against the problems. And there are a number of sensible solutions that could be implemented successfully if the professionals across the globe responsible for managing economic, political, and military affairs were given more leeway to devise and implement upgrades to the system.

The new administration in Washington takes a different view, of course. President Donald Trump never mentions the order and seems not to understand what it is or why it is a good thing. He appears to see the world in zero-sum terms—international politics as a Hobbesian war of all against all in which there are only deals, not relationships, and in which only relative gains matter. He combines this, moreover, with an acute sense of grievance—a conviction that everybody is winning at the United States' expense. "Every country takes advantage of us," he says, and notes that he intends to reverse the process.

No U.S. leader has talked this way in several generations, and most responsible officials in most countries, including the United States, are flummoxed—for they understand that if the White House actually tried to turn its more extreme ideas into policy, the entire system on which global security, stability, and prosperity is based would collapse.

Particularly shocked are the other members of the team—U.S. allies that have spent more than half a century believing American promises of open-ended support and basing their national policies on it. Does the president believe what he tweets, they ask? Are they official U.S. policy or a harbinger of it? The administration can send senior officials abroad to soothe nerves, walk back the heresies, and reassure everyone that the hegemon is not, in fact, planning to take its marbles and go home. But now that the unthinkable has been said, it will be hard to fully dispel the suspicion that Washington cannot be trusted to hold up its end of the bargain.

It is still early days for the Trump administration, and nobody knows what's going to happen next. Foreign Affairs will be covering this story in real time, both in print and online. But to set the stage for the ensuing drama, we offer this biography of the order's life to date, so readers can understand the stakes.

The collection begins with a great but long-forgotten essay from early 1943 by then editor Hamilton Fish Armstrong, capturing the period when the foreign policy establishment realized what needed to be done to win both the war and the peace that would follow. Next come excerpts from articles by various luminaries showing how different concepts and components of the order emerged—all emphasizing the importance, as Nelson Rockefeller puts it, of "widening the boundaries of national interest." Then (because life is short) the story jumps to the challenges and opportunities of the post–Cold War era, by which point the liberal order had spread around the globe and become the main game in town. The volume concludes with some discussion of what has happened since last November and what might follow.

Current global arrangements are not, in fact, "a mess," and so there will be substantial resistance from many quarters to any attempts to overturn them. So far the new administration has talked much but done little. And many of its senior officials are impressive professionals who fully understand the order's value. So the title and subtitle of this collection are exaggerated and alarmist. But they were chosen deliberately—to remind readers of how special and precious is the legacy today's policymakers have inherited, and of the damage that will be caused until Washington recovers its bearings.

Gideon Rose is Editor of Foreign Affairs.

© Foreign Affairs

Datum Point

Hamilton Fish Armstrong

OUR aim in this war is the complete material and psychological defeat of our enemies. We have rejected the idea of an armistice or negotiated peace and have pledged ourselves not to accept either at any stage or in any guise. When we have beaten Germany, Japan, Italy and their satellites, together or seriatim, into unconditional surrender, and while we are making sure that our accomplishment cannot be evaded or undone, we shall not recognize any limitations on our action except those imposed by our own consciences or any commitments except those which have been arrived at openly among the United Nations.

The outlines of the postwar world which we and our allies have already sketched constitute a pledge to and among ourselves alone. We may bungle the attempt to turn it into living reality. If so, we shall again suffer the lamentable consequences of our failure. But this time we are making our enemies no promises and shall not count on them to fulfill any part of a bargain. We on our side rely on ourselves alone—our own physical strength, our own strength of will. If we fail to keep the promises which we have made to ourselves and between ourselves we shall complete the destruction of our civilization by our own sole negligence and frivolity.

We hope to be able eventually to accept the peoples now our enemies as partners, and we are prepared to go as fast and as far as we safely can in making such a relationship with us seem reasonable and even attractive. But we fear that "eventually" is a long way off. In the interim, the one standard by which we shall measure every step will be whether it increases or diminishes our security. We shall try this time to remember how close we came to destruction and the grim sacrifices by which at the last moment we saved ourselves from it. Without vindictiveness but without apology or compunction we shall assign each of our beaten enemies his necessary rôle; and, provided we can match our perseverance to our present determination, we shall see that he carries that rôle through precisely, until such time as we may deliberately decide to modify it.

What does this mean, country by country?

It means that we intend to teach the German people beyond any chance of misunderstanding or later denial that they are not a race of supermen designated by some primordial decree to rule the world but instead a quite ordinary conglomeration of several racial stocks, without preternatural origins, with a number of unlovely traits as well as talents of a high order, and with a completely wrong belief that you can pound your neighbors into loving you as an apache pounds his woman into dazed rapture. We intend to see that the methods by which Germany regenerates herself confirm the lessons of her defeat. We hope that as a result of the dual demonstration Germans will understand that they are not unlike other nations and realize that in future they must cultivate something which they have always discounted in their attempts to wring satisfaction from an obscure destiny—the spontaneous esteem and collaboration of the rest of the world.

We are not so careless or unfair as to indict the whole German people for the specific crimes of some Germans. We do, however, indict them as a whole for having allowed arrogant thought and regardless action to secure a dominant place in their organized national life. We have only an academic interest in discussing whether the abdication of individual judgment which is responsible derives from a German inferiority complex or a German superiority complex, supposing the two are really different. We know that whichever it is, it has dogged the German people from the Valhalla of perpetual fights and feasts to the military councils of Potsdam, the beer halls of Munich, the frozen Volga and the grey village square where the French priest and postman are shot as a routine reprisal for some act of sabotage committed by persons unknown either to them or to the German officer who gives the command.

Some day, we must hope, the German nation will break loose from the ancient spell and cease to quiver between elation and despair, with acts of violence always the compensating outlet from either intolerable strain. Some day, we must hope, Wotan will yield to Apollo. Until we are sure that day has come we mean to curb at the source every manifestation of the traditional German spirit which can possibly bring ruin again to the quiet homes of peaceful peoples, near or far.

We do not underrate German culture, whether it comes to flower in German science or the glories of Goethe and Beethoven. Similarly, we think Germans should not underrate other cultures, and certainly not to the point where they feel entitled to tear them up by the roots and sow salt in the fields where they flourished. We cannot require Germans to think highly of Comenius or Chopin, Hus or Dvorak, Racine or Pasteur, Tolstoy or Tchaikovsky, Van Dyck or Erasmus; but we can require that they leave peoples which have produced men of genius like these to continue the peaceful enjoyment of their works and to continue adding diversifications and special beauties to our common civilization. We intend to do this. We recognize that we cannot reorient the German mentality from without by force or effect a lasting change in the political and social organization of German society against the will of the effective majority of Germans. But we can create conditions in the world which are likely to make the majority of Germans decide in favor of letting other nations continue to live well as a condition precedent to themselves living better. We have various plans whereby in the course of time and with sufficient good will we hope that all nations may be enabled to live better. So far as the Germans are concerned, we think we are likely to make permanent progress only if we address them at the start wholly in their own familiar categorical imperative:

"Conquered lands—leave them! Armies—disband them! Stolen goods—return them! Prisoners—free them! Discriminations—repeal them! War factories—dismantle them! Nazi heroes—hang them! Food? After we have fed those you have starved! Forgiveness? When you have repudiated the conception of German destiny which leads you to act detestably. Respect and confidence? When new German professors teach new lessons from new textbooks to new generations of German children, new German philosophers expound a new anti-mystic in new treatises, new editorial writers use a new language of tolerance in new German newspapers, new German statesmen seek a new German destiny in a new conception of coöperation and mutual accommodation, new German legislators embody that new conception in a new policy, new German judges ratify it, new German diplomats practise it and the German people in their hearts approve it!"

We intend to teach the Japanese, who have not been defeated in modern history, that they can be defeated. We intend to drive out of their heads the same fixed notion of superiority which makes the Germans feel thwarted and restless in any world not yet conquered. We intend to demonstrate to them that their Emperor is not a god but a man of most fallible judgment; that his policies are not evolved in the remote stillnesses of Heaven but in the councils of palace sycophants and ambitious generals; and that they are founded on error and bring disaster.

As with the Germans, we think the most hopeful way of giving the Japanese their new and necessary sense of proportion is by practical demonstration. No matter how long it takes, we shall reconquer from Japan bit by bit all the territories which she has seized in this and previous wars and return them to their inhabitants, either at once or so soon as they can develop, with our help, the necessary capacities for self-rule. We shall disarm Japan immediately and completely. Her neighbors will admit her to a share in the co-prosperity sphere of the Far East when they feel she no longer interprets that phrase as meaning prosperity for herself and slavery for others. She will be allowed to share in the discussions and decisions of civilized international society when the nations which have preserved that society from Axis depredations are convinced that she has definitely abandoned force as a national policy and will seek a proportioned destiny through negotiation and collaboration.

The lesson which the Italians must take to heart is simpler because they are intrinsically weaker. It is that a second-class Power cannot be built into a master race by rhetoric, grimaces, blackmail and castor oil, and that attempts to ride to conquest on the coat-tails of others will end in humiliation and disaster no matter which of the major contestants wins.

When we call Italians to account for their merciless conduct in Ethiopia, Spain, Greece and Jugoslavia we shall not forget that Leonardo and Dante enriched the whole human race or that a generous idealism burned, not for Italians alone, in the hearts of Mazzini and Garibaldi. Nor, on the other hand, shall we forget that the Italian sovereign acquiesced in the coup d'état of 1922 and in Mussolini's countless subsequent illegalities and that the Italian people, with a painfully small number of honorable exceptions, stood negligently by for 20 years while the Fascisti destroyed one after another of the liberties which Mazzini and Garibaldi had won them. We shall not forget how many Italians of ancient name and large fortune wore the Fascist badge lightly in their buttonholes while Black Shirt gunmen were murdering in the streets and Mussolini was defiling the monuments of antiquity with puerile scribblings. We have seen pictures of the Italian Army goose-stepping in imitation of the enemies their fathers expelled from Lombardy and Venetia. We still remember, now that Mussolini's conquests have been wiped from the map, how pleased most Italians were with them while they were being won easily and cheaply.

The record seems to require that we do more than welcome the Italian people's eleventh-hour repentance. Their pride in having established the first totalitarian state in modern Europe and their support or tolerance of its violence at home and aggression abroad through two decades constitute something more than a juvenile escapade. When the Nazis have been pushed beyond the Alps we must examine with great care to see whether the new spokesmen who come to us in Italy's name have clean hands and whether their past records confirm their professions of devotion to constitutional methods of government. We have no interest in rehabilitating individuals who gambled wrong and now would like to recoup their losses out of the supposedly abundant funds of American generosity and naïveté. Only Mussolini and the chiefs of his jackal pack will require bodily punishment. But many more must be excluded forever from all share in the direction of Italian affairs and any Italian government must remain for a time on probation.

We shall not forget the lesser culprits. Hungarians, Bulgars, Rumanians and others have sold their services and reputations to the Nazis and Fascists, in some cases in return for parcels of territory stolen from neighbors with whom they had just signed treaties of faithful friendship and mutual aid. To these also we intend to make a memorable demonstration on behalf of international law, order and good faith. They will, of course, disgorge their stolen goods completely. But it will not be sufficient for them to do that, to dismiss their puppet dictators, to hang the officials who have joined the invaders in committing so many atrocities, and to profess repentance. They must give evidence, through acts, that in future it will be much harder than it has been in the past for some great neighbor to bribe them, or for new leaders of their own to manœuvre them, into wasting the savings of their simple and hardworking populations in foreign wars. We hope through general security measures to forestall small as well as large breaches of the peace. Even so, we think that before the nations of Eastern Europe can collaborate peacefully several of them will have to modernize the present feudal structure of their society and that living conditions in that neighborhood will have to be improved and equalized both as between classes and between nations. Perhaps this can be achieved more easily if the nations in question come together in one or more confederations. We shall not impede any such development and we shall be ready to give what material aid we can in the execution of these necessary changes and improvements.

Presumably this statement of general intentions will be acceptable to most Americans. The differences of opinion crop out when one tries to particularize from the general, and especially when one begins to detail the lessons America must learn as well as those she must teach. Some people even feel quite sincerely that to think about those lessons or to outline the kind of world we are fighting for diverts energy from the fight itself and so constitutes a sort of sabotage.

There is, of course, a time for everything and first things come first. The American engineer dispatching a string of trucks northward from Zahidan, the marine landing at dawn on a beach on Guadalcanal, the pilot settling into the seat of his bomber for an attack on Düsseldorf, cannot be asked in that moment to think beyond the delivery into Russian hands of the tanks loaded on those trucks, the mopping up of the Japanese in the jungle behind that glimmering stretch of beach, the dropping of those bombs on the German factories. Nor can their colleagues back along the lines of communication to Washington and the officers there where operational directives are issued, spend time, while the day's work is still to be done, thinking about things outside their own spheres of responsibility. But there is nothing incompatible between doing the day's work and having a clear idea as to why it is necessary. In fact, people who are not professional soldiers are apt to do the day's work better if they understand clearly the reasons which make it necessary and the results which will be its justification. The definitions must be made for them, however, by their political leaders. This falls in their sphere of responsibility. They must see that the war is conducted not simply so that it is won in the quickest time and with the least loss of lives but also so that it secures the fullest possible achievement of our broadest national objectives.

The objectives of a nation are not marked by a dot in time; they are continuous and developing. Nobody can suppose that consideration of any temporary factors of numbers, technics or logistics kept England erect when Nazi bombs rocked Westminster and Buckingham Palace and turned Coventry and Bristol to rubble; or decided de Gaulle to quit his country, family and army and continue France's war against Germany; or sent Mihailovitch and his Serb guerrillas into the mountains to fight planes and cannon with knives and rifles; or made the Czech nation ignore threats and punishments and continue to strike as individuals against the soldiers and police of their conquerors; or collected a Polish army from Russian prisons to take up the war again in the Middle East; or informed the Russians that at Stalingrad they would be impregnable. In each of these peoples there was a conviction that in the substrata of its national being runs a vital current which is not finite and perishable but continuous and self-renewing and that it will supply future generations with the substance of a better life long after the fragments of enemy shells have rusted away in the ground. Each of them has imagination; but none could imagine a time when it would cease to exist or, existing, cease to grow.

The United States has inherited wellsprings of that same national confidence from the days of Plymouth Rock and Lewis and Clark and Ellis Island. The country then was not abashed by the unknown, could look at its lengthening shadow and say boldly: "I change because I grow." Today those springs are riled. Contradictions and uncertainties attend the convulsive efforts of a giant nation which has been sprawling at ease on the floor to send the right message to its unaccustomed muscles, to draw itself erect, to substitute disciplined action for uncontrolled reflexes, and to strike coördinated blows at the enemies who had assembled unnoticed to destroy it.

The springs must and can be cleared. They must be cleared, both because we need confidence that we can create a secure and at the same time growing society if we are to set about planning it with sufficient intelligence and energy, and because unless that confidence exists we shall find the purely military victory harder to win. They can be cleared, by defining aims which are reasonable and possible and by taking, in company with our allies, the preliminary steps which will permit giving those aims eventual realization. Doubts are being sown by pessimists and traitors. Fundamental American principles are being misinterpreted by those too timid to hold them intact. Monstrous world structures are being blueprinted by amateur engineers who seem to know everything except that nations are obstinately diverse. Milky illusions are being propagated by those who think of the war mainly as it seems to offer a lovely opportunity to transform the world into a neighborhood settlement house. And vague dreads and animosities are being inspired by those to whom it is only the opening phase of a new era of destructive social conflict and revolution. To such distortions the answer which will inspire confidence is not abuse, ridicule or violence but the presentation of a more detailed picture of our national destiny drawn on a larger canvas than any used yet.

The false prophets can be blanketed and the struggle in which we are engaged given more hopeful meaning if we will act imaginatively, yet soberly and with a sense of history, on the truth which Wendell Willkie uttered at Chungking: "The war is not simply a technical problem for tank forces; it is a war for men's minds." Since men's minds are not fettered by any limits of space or time our military strategy cannot accept such limits. When we repeat the current phrase that war is total, we mean—or ought to mean—that it is not merely total in its extent over the entire surface of the globe but total also in the inter-relation of what men remember from the past, what they do in the present and what they hope for the future.

It is a platitude of political discussion to say that a country should bring its responsibilities into balance with its physical powers. History furnishes plenty of horrifying examples of what happens, or might easily have happened, when it does not. But has the cardinal error of the United States been that it did not attempt to bring the two into balance? Does not history teach that the cardinal error of the United States was that it did not know where the line of its interests could be drawn?

The United States would be safe and respected, though hardly loved, if the whole area of its interests coincided with the zone of its power and if it remained constantly ready to use that power. But wishing will not make it so, and our adoption of a cautious policy of withdrawing our commitments to the outer limits of the range of our direct power will not protect those of our interests which lie beyond. It is beyond those limits, then, that foresight and the exercise of skill in the conduct of our foreign relations are most required. For it is in this outer zone that disputes which often do not seem to touch our interests originate and may grow into wars in which we may later be forced involuntarily to intervene. That outer zone, the writer believes, has no limits in the whole world.

If this thesis is true, we need urgently to arrange for our influence to be felt everywhere in the world, continuously and hence in time, despite the fact that in many parts of it we are unable to exercise power directly. And for this purpose we must accept partnership in a system of give and take, called by President Beneš "live and help live," not on a limited basis calculated by the limited range of our own individual power but on a universal basis calculated by the unlimited range of our national interest.

With whom shall we deal? With the nations that happen to live in our neighborhood, and as the leader of this bloc with other regional blocs? Or with one or two or three other Great Powers which in turn can exercise control over large areas of the world, so that together we can in fact control it all? Or with all like-minded Powers, the more the better? The writer believes that in the long run the United States will be stronger and safer in the larger group than in a bloc or a limited alliance. He believes that the general acceptance of a general relationship, with general though graduated responsibilities, offers the only basis for organizing world peace under the conditions produced by the development of science, communication and education, and that nothing but world peace is good enough for a World Power like the United States.

The cautious will say that half a loaf is better than no bread. But if the half loaf is not enough to support life, it is not worth risking much to gain. The American people will not find sufficient reward for their present sacrifices in being enabled to escape responsibility for helping prevent several small wars and then either perish or lose their way of life in another great war.

Neville Chamberlain said that the British people were not concerned with what was happening in a faraway land. As a result of that misapprehension Britain came as near to perishing as a nation can come and still manage to survive; and if Britain had perished we also should have perished, in one sense or another of the word. There is no faraway land. Our struggle to fix that fact in the public consciousness must not cease or falter. We must not proffer the American people half loaves or plan to accept half loaves on their behalf. On a half loaf they can subsist temporarily; they cannot live securely, nor develop as a nation the collective characteristics which in an individual we recognize give proportion, harmony and lasting satisfaction.

These pages are written in the conviction that our national future is bound up with the future of the whole world and not any single part of it; that it is possible at one time to learn from the past, work in the present and look to the future; and that it is necessary for our salvation that we do these three things together, do them on the scale indicated, and do them now.

Without a military victory there is no chance of a worthy peace. Without a worthy peace victory will have been worth winning in only a very limited sense. Whether or not the peace is worthy will depend on the coördinated action and common will of the United Nations—all of them—now and later. Unless we can reach clear understandings among ourselves now we are most unlikely to get them later. For the pattern of any future organization of the world will derive from the habits and instruments we create to deal with our present common peril, and if we cannot agree when the peril is instant and concrete how shall we agree when it has resumed the appearance of an abstraction?

These ideas are throbbing in the minds of millions of Americans, military and civilian alike, even as they concentrate on the day-by-day problems of the war. They crave to be told what it is they will get out of victory besides temporary survival. To let them see what they will get if they will assume the risks of peace as firmly as they have assumed the risks of war is not to divert their energies from the fearful tasks in hand—to give them, as one commentator naïvely put it, an opiate. On the contrary, it is to throw idle dynamos into action.

"From a high hill near the airdrome," wrote Byron Darnton from New Guinea in a last dispatch to the New York Times before his death there on October 18, 1942, "a man can see his countrymen building with blood, sweat and toil the firm resolution that their sons shall not die under bombs but shall have peace, because they will know how to preserve peace." Let the resolution of men at desks match the resolution of men under bombs. And let it be a resolution informed by the failures of the past and measuring without either foolish optimism or needless despair the difficulties and hazards of the future.

HAMILTON FISH ARMSTRONG, editor of FOREIGN AFFAIRS

The Economic Tasks of the Postwar World [Excerpt]

Alvin H. Hansen and C. P. Kindleberger

Roosevelt and Churchill aboard HMS Prince of Wales.

... There are still a good many people deeply concerned with problems of international security who think exclusively in terms of political arrangements and economic mechanisms such as tariffs and currencies. We would call that the passive approach. The arrangements and mechanisms which they favor are important, and appropriate means must be found to give them effect. But many economists are coming to think that action along these traditional lines would by itself be wholly inadequate. It is increasingly understood that the essential foundation upon which the international security of the future must be built is an economic order so managed and controlled that it will be capable of sustaining full employment and developing a rising standard of living as rapidly as technical progress and world productivity will permit. The very survival of our present institutions, including political democracy and private enterprise, depends upon our taking a bolder attitude toward public developmental projects in terms both of human and physical resources, and both in our own country and throughout the world.

Many questions at once arise. What will be the rôle of government in postwar economic life? Will business enterprise outside of government be organized predominantly along cartel lines, with increasing restraints on competition? Will international trade be based on principles of nondiscrimination or will each country make the best bargains it can obtain on a bilateral and separate basis with each of its trading partners? Will the world break up into autarchic countries, pairs of countries, or regions, including empires, continents and hemispheres? Or will each country tend to specialize in the production of those particular commodities which it can produce most efficiently and trade on the widest possible basis?

These questions are practical ones, and like most practical questions it is impossible to answer them categorically either as a forecast of the future or as a guide to desirable policy under the unforeseeable conditions of the future. It can merely be said that in time of war governments must and do assume more direction of economic life; that after this war they will probably be given increased responsibility for trying to get rid of unemployment in their respective nations and to establish higher minimum standards for the low-income groups; and that while the degree of control exercised in the postwar period will be less than that exercised during the war, it nevertheless will be greater than it used to be before the war. ... [Full article]

ALVIN H. HANSEN, Littauer Professor of Political Economy at Harvard University; special economic adviser, Board of Governors of the Federal Reserve System; American chairman of the Joint Economic Committee of Canada and the United States; author of "Economic Stabilization in an Unbalanced World," "Fiscal Policy and Business Cycles" and other works; C. P. KINDLEBERGER, Associate Economist, Board of Governors of the Federal Reserve System; author of "International Short-Term Capital Movement"

Bretton Woods and International Cooperation [Excerpt]

Henry Morgenthau Jr.

Mount Washington Hotel, Bretton Woods, 1905.

THE United Nations won a great if unheralded victory at the Bretton Woods Monetary and Financial Conference. For they took the first, the most vital and the most difficult step toward putting into effect the sort of international economic program which will be necessary for preserving the peace and creating favorable conditions for world prosperity.

International agreements in the monetary and financial field are admittedly hard to reach, since they lie at the very heart of matters affecting the whole complex system of economic relations among nations. It is a familiar fact that in all countries sectional interests are often in conflict with the broader national interests and that these narrow interests are sometimes sufficiently strong to shape international economic policy. It was, therefore, a special source of satisfaction to all the participants in the Conference that agreements were reached covering so wide a range of international monetary and financial problems. This was largely due to long and careful preparation preceding the Conference during which we secured general recognition of the principle of international monetary and financial coöperation.

The Conference of 44 nations prepared Articles of Agreement for establishing the International Monetary Fund and the International Bank for Reconstruction and Development to provide the means for consultation and collaboration on international monetary and investment problems. These agreements demonstrate that the United Nations have the willingness and the ability to unite on the most difficult economic issues, issues on which comprehensive agreement had never before been reached even among countries with essentially similar political and economic institutions. The victory was thus all the greater in that the Bretton Woods Agreements were prepared by countries of differing degrees of economic development, with very far from similar economic systems, and will operate not merely in the immediate postwar years, as will UNRRA, but in the longer period ahead.

The hope that the United Nations will not prove a merely temporary wartime coalition which will disintegrate after military victory has thus received substantial reinforcement. No matter what pattern future organs of international coöperation may assume—and the pattern may be diverse and varied to correspond with the great variety of problems to be met—Bretton Woods proved that if the determination to coöperate for peace as well as for war is present, adequate and suitable instruments can be devised in every sphere where international action is needed. In that sense, Bretton Woods was an unmistakable warning to the Axis that the United Nations cannot be divided either by military force or by the diplomatic intrigues of our enemies. It gave an unequivocal assurance to the soldiers of the United Nations that the sacrifices they are making to stamp out forever the causes of war are not being made in vain. And lastly it was a sign to the civilians on whose labors the war efforts of all the United Nations depend that such labors are bearing fruit in the councils of peace no less than those of war.

I have indicated that at Bretton Woods the United Nations took the first and hardest step toward the adoption of the kind of economic program necessary for world stability and prosperity. It was only the first step because the Articles of Agreement for the establishment of the Fund and the Bank still have to be ratified by each of the participants in accordance with legal and constitutional requirements and procedures. I would be the last to claim that the process is likely to be a simple or an easy one. Yet, so far as the action to be taken by the United States is concerned, I have sufficient faith in the common sense of the American people to believe that they have learned the painful lesson that the best way to guard our national interests is through effective international coöperation. We know that much remains to be done in other fields. But, despite their highly technical nature, the Fund and the Bank are the best starting point for international economic coöperation, because lack of agreement in these spheres would bedevil all other world economic relations.

Highly technical questions have one great advantage from the political point of view—their very intricacy should raise them above merely partisan considerations. My optimism is partly based on the belief that the Bretton Woods proposals will be discussed on an objective basis and that such differences of opinion as may emerge will not follow party lines. The American delegation was non-partisan in composition and was thoroughly united on all major questions. Republicans and Democrats alike had an equal voice in shaping its decisions, and there is good reason to expect that the precedent followed before and during the Conference will be continued and that the next stage of ratification will be conducted on the same high plane. In the light of my experience as chairman of the American delegation, I believe that men of broad vision in both parties will rise to the challenge and the opportunity to initiate the historical pattern of international economic coöperation that world peace demands. The challenge and opportunity are all the greater because our course of action will largely determine the course of action of many other members of the United Nations. "As America goes, so goes the world" may be an exaggeration. But it is a pardonable exaggeration in a world made one by time and fate, in which America's strength and potentialities are perhaps more clearly realized by the rest of the world than by the American people itself. I should therefore like to emphasize as strongly as possible that a tremendous responsibility rests on our government and people in connection with the ratification of the Bretton Woods Agreements. For our action will be rightly or wrongly interpreted as a sure and infallible index of our intentions with respect to the shape of things to come.

II

The fate of the Treaty of Versailles adds to the significance of the course we adopt on the Bretton Woods proposals. As the President has pointed out, the Allied leaders are acquainted with our constitutional processes as they affect our dealings with foreign powers. If there are any Americans who would utilize the division of powers to defeat the ends sought by the vast majority of Americans, they are not likely to succeed if the issues are clearly and unambiguously presented to the Congress and the people. We must always keep in mind that other nations are anxiously asking whether the United States has the desire and ability to coöperate effectively in establishing world peace. If we fail to ratify the Bretton Woods Agreements, they will be convinced that the American people either do not desire to coöperate or that they do not know how to achieve coöperation. They would then have little alternative but to seek a solution for their pressing political and economic problems on the old familiar lines, lines which will inexorably involve playing the old game of power politics with even greater intensity than before because the problems with which they will be confronted will be so much more acute. And power politics would be as disastrous to prosperity as to peace.

One important reason for the sharp decline in international trade in the 1930's and the spread of depression from country to country was the growth of the twin evils of international economic aggression and monetary disorder. The decade of the 1930's was almost unique in the multiplicity of ingenious schemes that were devised by some countries, notably Germany, to exploit their creditors, their customers, and their competitors in their international trade and financial relations. It is necessary only to recall the use of exchange controls, competitive currency depreciation, multiple currency practices, blocked balances, bilateral clearing arrangements and the host of other restrictive and discriminatory devices to find the causes for the inadequate recovery in international trade in the decade before the war. These monetary devices were measures of international economic aggression, and they were the logical concomitant of a policy directed toward war and conquest.

The postwar international economic problems may well be more difficult than those of the 1930's, and unless we coöperate to solve these problems, we may be faced with a resumption and intensification of monetary disorder and economic aggression in the postwar period. There is no need to enlarge on the consequences of such a development. It is a bleak prospect, yet it is one we must understand. In some countries it will present itself as the only practical alternative if the rest of the world should be unable to count on effective American participation in a rounded and coherent program covering international political and economic relations. If that should come to pass, we will have to frame our own future to fit a world in which war will never be a remote contingency and in which economic barriers and restrictions will be the rule in a contracting economic universe. On the other hand, if we ratify the Bretton Woods Agreements, we will be showing the rest of the world not only that we can coöperate for winning the war, not only that we are capable of formulating a program for fulfilling our common aspirations, but that we intend to enforce and implement such a program in every relevant sphere of action. Ratification would thus strengthen all the forward-looking elements in every country who wish to translate their craving for peace into deeds and will be a resounding answer to the pessimists who feel that peace is unattainable.

The institution of an international security organization on the lines agreed on at Dumbarton Oaks constitutes a history-making accomplishment of which we may well be proud. Here is an organization for maintaining peace and political security which for the first time has teeth in it. But it is our duty to keep to a minimum the tensions to which that organization will be subjected and to deal with the economic causes of aggression before the stage is reached where more far-reaching measures would be necessary. International monetary and financial coöperation is indispensable for the maintenance of economic stability; and economic stability, in turn, is indispensable to the maintenance of political stability. Therefore, a program for international economic coöperation of which Bretton Woods is the first step must accompany the program for political and military security toward which the United Nations are moving. Bretton Woods is the model in the economic sphere of what Dumbarton Oaks is in the political. They reinforce and supplement each other. Political and economic security from aggression are indivisible, and a sound program for peace must achieve both.

...

[Full Article]

HENRY MORGENTHAU, JR., Secretary of the Treasury

© Foreign Affairs

The Illusion of World Government [Excerpt]

Reinhold Niebuhr

Representatives of 26 United Nations attend Flag Day ceremonies in the White House in 1942.

THE trustful acceptance of false solutions for our perplexing problems adds a touch of pathos to the tragedy of our age.

The tragic character of our age is revealed in the world-wide insecurity which is the fate of modern man. Technical achievements, which a previous generation had believed capable of solving every ill to which the human flesh is heir, have created, or at least accentuated, our insecurity. For the growth of technics has given the perennial problems of our common life a more complex form and a scope that has grown to be world-wide.

Our problem is that technics have established a rudimentary world community but have not integrated it organically, morally or politically. They have created a community of mutual dependence, but not one of mutual trust and respect. Without this higher integration, advancing technics tend to sharpen economic rivalries within a general framework of economic interdependence; they change the ocean barriers of yesterday into the battlegrounds of today; and they increase the deadly efficacy of the instruments of war so that vicious circles of mutual fear may end in atomic conflicts and mutual destruction. To these perplexities an ideological conflict has been added, which divides the world into hostile camps.

It is both necessary and laudable that men of good will should, in this situation, seek to strengthen every moral and political force which might give a rudimentary world community a higher degree of integration. It was probably inevitable that the desperate plight of our age should persuade some well meaning men that the gap between a technically integrated and politically divided community could be closed by the simple expedient of establishing a world government through the fiat of the human will and creating world community by the fiat of world government. It is this hope which adds a touch of pathos to already tragic experiences. The hope not only beguiles some men from urgent moral and political responsibilities. It tempts others into irresponsible criticisms of the necessarily minimal constitutional structure which we have embodied in the United Nations and which is as bad as its critics aver only if a better one is within the realm of possibilities.

Virtually all arguments for world government rest upon the simple presupposition that the desirability of world order proves the attainability of world government. Our precarious situation is unfortunately no proof, either of the moral ability of mankind to create a world government by an act of the will, nor of the political ability of such a government to integrate a world community in advance of a more gradual growth of the "social tissue" which every community requires more than government.

Most advocates of world government also assume that nations need merely follow the alleged example of the individuals of another age who are supposed to have achieved community by codifying their agreements into law and by providing an agency of some kind for law enforcement. This assumption ignores the historic fact that the mutual respect for each other's rights in particular communities is older than any code of law; and that machinery for the enforcement of law can be efficacious only when a community as a whole obeys its laws implicitly, so that coercive enforcement may be limited to a recalcitrant minority.

The fallacy of world government can be stated in two simple propositions. The first is that governments are not created by fiat (though sometimes they can be imposed by tyranny). The second is that governments have only limited efficacy in integrating a community... .

... In short, the forces which are operating to integrate the world community are limited. To call attention to this fact does not mean that all striving for a higher and wider integration of the world community is vain. That task must and will engage the conscience of mankind for ages to come. But the edifice of government which we build will be sound and useful if its height is proportionate to the strength of the materials from which it is constructed. The immediate political situation requires that we seek not only peace, but also the preservation of a civilization which we hold to be preferable to the universal tyranny with which Soviet aggression threatens us. Success in this double task is the goal; let us not be diverted from it by the pretense that there is a simple alternative.... . [Full Article]

REINHOLD NIEBUHR, Professor of Applied Christianity in the Union Theological Seminary, New York; author of many works on philosophical, religious and political subjects, the latest of them "Faith and History"

Widening Boundaries of National Interest [Excerpt]

Nelson A. Rockefeller

Truman's inaugural address, 1949.

IN A few paragraphs, the fourth point of President Truman's inaugural address in January 1949 phrased a concept that sparked an electric response along the great circuit that links the minds and imaginations of human beings throughout the world. The concept was basically simple. It declared that:

1. Mankind for the first time in history possesses the knowledge and skills to make his environment yield an adequate and progressively improving return to all peoples.

2. Despite this knowledge, more than half of the world's people still live under economic systems which provide less than minimum needs of food, clothing and shelter, and lack the promise of betterment.

3. Since the security and continued prosperity of the United States and other relatively industrialized nations can be maintained only if there is complementary progress in the economically backward areas, we should assume the leadership in a concerted productive effort which will promote both their interests and ours.

4. Basic to the accomplishment of this purpose is a flow of investment capital, carrying with it technical and managerial skills, to create and harness mechanical power and production tools and equipment so that they supplement the work of human muscles. Our policy should focus on creating conditions that permit and encourage such transfers, under procedures that avoid imperialism or any form of exploitation on either side, and are founded upon mutual respect and recognition of a mutual interest.

5. "Democracy alone can supply the vitalizing force to stir the peoples of the world into triumphant action, not only against their human oppressors, but also against their ancient enemies—hunger, misery and despair."

The wide and extraordinarily warm response invoked everywhere outside of the Communist world by this formulation of a new phase of American foreign policy merits examination. Seemingly, it stemmed in part from a recognition that we were thereby taking a further step away from our traditional isolationism. Our acceptance of a common interest between United States and Western Europe had been attested by our participation in two world wars and by direct military and economic aid, amounting to some 55 billion dollars, given to Europe during and after the second of these struggles. Point Four was a declaration that our interest included a concern for the well-being and progress of the entire world.

Furthermore, this interest was defined not in military or even in political terms. The pronouncement placed it squarely upon economic considerations that linked the continuing progress of our system to a correlative development in the economies of all democratic peoples. As a nation, we have 6 percent of the world's peoples and 7 percent of the world's land area, but more than half of the world's industrial output. Yet we possess only one-third of the raw materials, so that we depend upon others for a large part of our strength. These economic ties have a way of persisting through periods of peace, war or the uneasy half-war, half-peace, in which the world now lives.

Thus, the principles stated in Point Four were accepted as an assurance that we have moved from self-contained sufficiency to a recognition of our responsible partnership in a free-world effort. This emphasis has tremendous import. Its implications should be thoroughly understood here as well as abroad.

There already was no lack of evidence that the United States stood ready to coöperate with other nations in time of need. Over the past ten years the total of its military and economic assistance to other nations has amounted to the staggering sum of approximately 80 billion dollars. But the money was spent for emergency measures to meet successive crises. One after another, lend-lease, UNRRA, the United Kingdom loan, Philippine rehabilitation, Greek and Turkish, Japanese and Korean aid, the Economic Recovery Program, and even to a major degree our subscriptions to the International Bank and Monetary Fund arrangements agreed upon at Bretton Woods—each was submitted to and accepted by the people of the United States as something that must be done to avoid catastrophe, with a strong implication that once it was done the situation would be well in hand and our responsibilities discharged.

It is unfortunate that the presentation of the Point Four concept to the American public and the specific steps implementing it have taken a form that carries the dual connotation of a "give-away program" and one that is principally concerned with sending technicians abroad to offer advice. Humanitarian motives are deeply ingrained in the United States tradition and have been nourished by the religious and democratic heritage of its people. But the tendency to accept the giving of grants and advice as an all-embracing definition of what is implied in the Point Four program does a major disservice to its basic principles.

Such an interpretation narrows the broad pronouncement of community of interests put forth in the President's original statement, and it even now clearly whittles down the statement of purpose given to the program by Congress in Title IV of its Act for International Development (Public Law 535). In Section 403(a) of this law, Congress states: "It is declared to be the policy of the United States to aid the efforts of the peoples of economically underdeveloped areas to develop their resources and improve their working and living conditions by encouraging the exchange of technical knowledge and skills and the flow of investment capital to countries which provide conditions under which such technical assistance and capital can effectively and constructively contribute to raising standards of living, creating new sources of wealth, increasing productivity and expanding purchasing power." In a preceding paragraph [Section 402 (a)] it is stated: "The peoples of the United States and other nations have a common interest in freedom and in the economic progress of all peoples. Such progress can further the secure growth of democratic ways of life, the expansion of mutually beneficial commerce, the development of international understanding and good will, and the maintenance of world peace."

It is this emphasis upon community of interests that gives significance to Point Four as an important forward step in the evolution of our foreign policy. Once accepted, it is clear that any program for carrying out our intent must be broad enough to embrace all of the aspects in which our economy exerts important impacts upon the economies of others in the free world, not merely the giving of gifts and technical advice. It is equally clear that the program must be a continuing one-geared to the deliberate pace of economic development rather than to the bell-clanging rush of apparatus designed to put out fires.

The pressure of compelling political or security considerations will necessarily change the focus and the emphasis of our economic policies at home and abroad. The policy of Soviet Russia and her dominated satellites is to organize a tightly-contained economic area having the least possible trade with free-world areas. This necessarily restricts our community of economic interest to those countries outside the Soviet orbit. The militarily aggressive Soviet policy forces us at the present time to give precedence at home and abroad to those aspects of economic activity which will assure successful resistance to that aggression either through direct production of armaments or through correcting deficiencies that make certain areas peculiarly vulnerable to pressure from without or subversion from within.

But the aim of our foreign economic policy should remain constant—in peace, in emergency, or in war, if war cannot be avoided. If we live up to our pronouncements, we shall conduct our economic affairs as a whole in a way to further the healthy, balanced development and the progressively larger yield of the economies of all peoples who elect to belong to the free-world trading system.

II

...

If we look beyond the present emergency to our long-term economic prospects we see that the stake of the United States and Western Europe in an expanding economy throughout the free world is even more impressive. The United States accounts for more than one-half of the heavy industry production of the world, but it mines only about a third of the 15 basic minerals upon which such production depends. Even so, it is depleting its mineral reserves at an exorbitant rate. On balance, the mineral reserves now within Soviet Russia's effective control are larger than those available to the United States within her own borders and from other parts of the Western Hemisphere. Our industry will become increasingly dependent upon imports. If access to the raw materials of the underdeveloped areas were to be denied to us and to Western Europe, our current industrial outputs would be devastatingly affected. Unless development in those areas keeps pace, it simply will not be possible for the United States and Western Europe to continue to expand their economies in the future in the manner which has given them their strength in the past.

Thus both the security of our free world and our own continuing economic growth are dependent upon the development of the underdeveloped countries. But we should be under no illusions that we could, even if we wanted, expand them as raw material suppliers exclusively, retaining ourselves the more lucrative operations of transferring such materials into manufactures. The history of the United States shows conclusively how stubbornly the people of a nation and of its several segments insist upon the prerogative of diversification, and how wise they are to do so.

Thus while we must seek to expand the free world's raw material production, our policy must be sufficiently broad and sufficiently wise to encourage an industrial expansion as well. The chief incentive of the underdeveloped areas to produce additional raw materials for export will be the desire to acquire the exchange to purchase the equipment for building healthily-balanced economies. Initially they must purchase such heavy equipment from industrialized areas, since machine tools and machinery generally are the product of relatively mature economies. Eventually, they will produce such machines themselves. Those who fear the impact of such competition would do well to consider the volume of market demand if the billion people of the underdeveloped free-world areas could raise their per capita incomes from the present average of $80 per year to the $473 level of Western Europe or to the $1,453 level of the United States.

. . .

V

. . . If 3 billion dollars annually were directed wisely into crucially productive channels, if it were supplemented by additional grants or investments from other relatively advanced economies, if our procurement and export policies are handled with due regard to the interests of the whole free world—the tempo of economic advance in the areas in question would be, in truth, revolutionized. The hope of discernible progress would replace the despair of stagnation. And we should have gone far toward giving meaning to the institutions of democracy, and a sense of a living and deepening community of interest to free nations. [Full Article]

NELSON A. ROCKEFELLER, Chairman of the International Development Advisory Board; Coördinator of Inter-American Affairs, 1940-45; Assistant Secretary of State, 1944-45

The Myth of Post–Cold War Chaos [Excerpt]

G. John Ikenberry

The Berlin Wall, 1986.

A great deal of ink has been shed in recent years describing various versions of the post-Cold War order. These attempts have all failed, because there is no such creature. The world order created in the 1940s is still with us, and in many ways stronger than ever. The challenge for American foreign policy is not to imagine and build a new world order but to reclaim and renew an old one—an innovative and durable order that has been hugely successful and largely unheralded.

The end of the Cold War, the common wisdom holds, was a historical watershed. The collapse of communism brought the collapse of the order that took shape after World War II. While foreign policy theorists and officials scramble to design new grand strategies, the United States is rudderless on uncharted seas.

The common wisdom is wrong. What ended with the Cold War was bipolarity, the nuclear stalemate, and decades of containment of the Soviet Union—seemingly the most dramatic and consequential features of the postwar era. But the world order created in the middle to late 1940s endures, more extensive and in some respects more robust than during its Cold War years. Its basic principles, which deal with organization and relations among the Western liberal democracies, are alive and well.

These less celebrated, less heroic, but more fundamental principles and policies—the real international order—include the commitment to an open world economy and its multilateral management, and the stabilization of socioeconomic welfare. And the political vision behind the order was as important as the anticipated economic gains. The major industrial democracies took it upon themselves to "domesticate" their dealings through a dense web of multilateral institutions, intergovernmental relations, and joint management of the Western and world political economies.... .

World War II produced two postwar settlements. One, a reaction to deteriorating relations with the Soviet Union, led to the containment order, which was based on the balance of power, nuclear deterrence, and political and ideological competition. The other, a reaction to the economic rivalry and political turmoil of the 1930s and the resulting world war, can be called the liberal democratic order. It culminated in a wide range of new institutions and relations among the Western industrial democracies, built around economic openness, political reciprocity, and multilateral management of an American-led liberal political system.... .

... The liberal democratic agenda was less obviously a grand strategy designed to advance American security interests [than was containment], and it was inevitably viewed during the Cold War as secondary, a preoccupation of economists and businessmen. The policies and institutions that supported free trade among the advanced industrial societies seemed the stuff of low politics. But the liberal democratic agenda was actually built on a robust yet sophisticated set of ideas about American security interests, the causes of war and depression, and a desirable postwar political order.... .

The most basic conviction underlying the postwar liberal agenda was that the closed autarkic regions that had contributed to the worldwide depression and split the globe into competing blocs before the war must be broken up and replaced by an open, nondiscriminatory economic system. Peace and security, proponents had decided, were impossible in the face of exclusive economic regions. The challengers of liberal multilateralism, however, occupied almost every corner of the advanced industrial world. Germany and Japan were the most overtly hostile; both had pursued a dangerous path that combined authoritarian capitalism with military dictatorship and coercive regional autarky. But the British Commonwealth and its imperial preference system also challenged liberal multilateral order.

The hastily drafted Atlantic Charter was an American effort to ensure that Britain signed on to its liberal democratic war aims. The joint statement of principles affirmed free trade, equal access to natural resources for all interested buyers, and international economic collaboration to advance labor standards, employment security, and social welfare. Roosevelt and Churchill declared before the world that they had learned the lessons of the interwar years—and those lessons were fundamentally about the proper organization of the Western political economy. America's enemies, its friends, and even America itself had to be reformed and integrated into the postwar economic system.

The postwar liberal democratic order was designed to solve the internal problems of Western industrial capitalism. It was not intended to fight Soviet communism, nor was it simply a plan to get American business back on its feet after the war by opening up the world to trade and investment. It was a strategy to build Western solidarity through economic openness and joint political governance. Four principles pursued in the 1940s gave shape to this order.

The most obvious principle was economic openness, which would ideally take the form of a system of nondiscriminatory trade and investment.... . American thinking was that economic openness was an essential element of a stable and peaceful world political order. "Prosperous neighbors are the best neighbors," remarked Roosevelt administration Treasury official Harry Dexter White. But officials were convinced that American economic and security interests demanded it as well. Great liberal visionaries and hard-nosed geopolitical strategists could agree on the notion of open markets; it united American postwar planners and was the seminal idea informing the work of the Bretton Woods conference on postwar economic cooperation.... .

The second principle was joint management of the Western political-economic order. The leading industrial democratic states must not only lower barriers to trade and the movement of capital but must govern the system. This also was a lesson from the 1930s: institutions, rules, and active mutual management by governments were necessary to avoid unproductively competitive and conflictual economic practices. Americans believed such cooperation necessary in a world where national economies were increasingly at the mercy of developments abroad. The unwise or untoward policies of one country threatened contagion, undermining the stability of all. As Roosevelt said at the opening of Bretton Woods, "The economic health of every country is a proper matter of concern to all its neighbors, near and far." ...

A third principle of liberal democratic order held that the rules and institutions of the Western world economy must be organized to support domestic economic stability and social security. This new commitment was foreshadowed in the Atlantic Charter's call for postwar international collaboration to ensure employment stability and social welfare. It was a sign of the times that Churchill, a conservative Tory, could promise a historic expansion of the government's responsibility for the people's well-being. In their schemes for postwar economic order, both Britain and the United States sought a system that would aid and protect their nascent social and economic commitments. They wanted an open world economy, but one congenial to the emerging welfare state as well as business.

The discovery of a middle way between old political alternatives was a major innovation of the postwar Western economic order. British and American planners began their discussion in 1942 deadlocked, Britain's desire for full employment and economic stabilization after the war running up against the American desire for free trade. The breakthrough came in 1944 with the Bretton Woods agreements on monetary order, which secured a more or less open system of trade and payments while providing safeguards for domestic economic stability through the International Monetary Fund. The settlement was a synthesis that could attract a new coalition of conservative free traders and the liberal prophets of economic planning.

A final element of the liberal democratic system might be termed "constitutionalism"—meaning simply that the Western nations would make systematic efforts to anchor their joint commitments in principled and binding institutional mechanisms. In fact, this may be the order's most basic aspect, encompassing the other principles and policies and giving the whole its distinctive domestic character. Governments might ordinarily seek to keep their options open, cooperating with other states but retaining the possibility of disengagement. The United States and the other Western nations after the war did exactly the opposite. They built long-term economic, political, and security commitments that were difficult to retract, and locked in the relationships, to the extent that sovereign states can... .

For those who thought cooperation among the advanced industrial democracies was driven primarily by Cold War threats, the last few years must appear puzzling. Relations between the major Western countries have not broken down. Germany has not rearmed, nor has Japan. What the Cold War focus misses is an appreciation of the other, less heralded, postwar American project—the building of a liberal order in the West. Archaeologists remove one stratum only to discover an older one beneath; the end of the Cold War allows us to see a deeper and more enduring layer of the postwar political order that was largely obscured by the more dramatic struggles between East and West.

Fifty years after its founding, the Western liberal democratic world is robust, and its principles and policies remain the core of world order. The challenges to liberal multilateralism both from within and from outside the West have mainly disappeared. Although regional experiments abound, they are fundamentally different from the autarkic blocs of the 1930s. The forces of business and financial integration are moving the globe inexorably toward a more tightly interconnected system that ignores regional as well as national borders... .

Some aspects of the vision of the 1940s have faded. The optimism about government activism and economic management that animated the New Deal and Keynesianism has been considerably tempered. Likewise, the rule-based, quasi-judicial functions of liberal multilateralism have eroded, particularly in monetary relations. Paradoxically, although the rules of cooperation have become less coherent, cooperation itself has increased. Formal rules governing the Western world economy have gradually been replaced by a convergence of thinking on economic policy. The consensus on the broad outlines of desirable domestic and international economic policies has both reflected and promoted increased economic growth and the incorporation of emerging economies into the system.

The problems the liberal democratic order confronts are mostly problems of success, foremost among them the need to integrate the newly developing and post-communist countries. Here one sees most clearly that the post-Cold War order is really a continuation and extension of the Western order forged during and after World War II. The difference is its increasingly global reach. The world has seen an explosion in the desire of countries and peoples to move toward democracy and capitalism. When the history of the late twentieth century is written, it will be the struggle for more open and democratic polities throughout the world that will mark the era, rather than the failure of communism.

Other challenges to the system are boiling up in its leading states. In its early years, rapid and widely shared economic growth buoyed the system, as working- and middle-class citizens across the advanced industrial world rode the crest of the boom. Today economic globalization is producing much greater inequality between the winners and the losers, the wealthy and the poor. How the subsequent dislocations, dashed expectations, and political grievances are dealt with—whether the benefits are shared and the system as a whole is seen as socially just—will affect the stability of the liberal world order more than regional conflict.... . [Full Article]

G. JOHN IKENBERRY *is Co-Director of the Lauder Institute of Management and International Studies and Associate Professor of Political Science at the University of Pennsylvania.*

The Real New World Order

Anne-Marie Slaughter

THE STATE STRIKES BACK

Many thought that the new world order proclaimed by George Bush was the promise of 1945 fulfilled, a world in which international institutions, led by the United Nations, guaranteed international peace and security with the active support of the world's major powers. That world order is a chimera. Even as a liberal internationalist ideal, it is infeasible at best and dangerous at worst. It requires a centralized rule-making authority, a hierarchy of institutions, and universal membership. Equally to the point, efforts to create such an order have failed. The United Nations cannot function effectively independent of the major powers that compose it, nor will those nations cede their power and sovereignty to an international institution. Efforts to expand supranational authority, whether by the U.N. secretary-general's office, the European Commission, or the World Trade Organization (WTO), have consistently produced a backlash among member states.

The leading alternative to liberal internationalism is "the new medievalism," a back-to-the-future model of the 21st century. Where liberal internationalists see a need for international rules and institutions to solve states' problems, the new medievalists proclaim the end of the nation-state. Less hyperbolically, in her article, "Power Shift," in the January/February 1997 Foreign Affairs, Jessica T. Mathews describes a shift away from the state—up, down, and sideways—to supra-state, sub-state, and, above all, nonstate actors. These new players have multiple allegiances and global reach.

Mathews attributes this power shift to a change in the structure of organizations: from hierarchies to networks, from centralized compulsion to voluntary association. The engine of this transformation is the information technology revolution, a radically expanded communications capacity that empowers individuals and groups while diminishing traditional authority. The result is not world government, but global governance. If government denotes the formal exercise of power by established institutions, governance denotes cooperative problem-solving by a changing and often uncertain cast. The result is a world order in which global governance networks link Microsoft, the Roman Catholic Church, and Amnesty International to the European Union, the United Nations, and Catalonia.

The new medievalists miss two central points. First, private power is still no substitute for state power. Consumer boycotts of transnational corporations destroying rain forests or exploiting child labor may have an impact on the margin, but most environmentalists or labor activists would prefer national legislation mandating control of foreign subsidiaries. Second, the power shift is not a zero-sum game. A gain in power by nonstate actors does not necessarily translate into a loss of power for the state. On the contrary, many of these nongovernmental organizations (ngos) network with their foreign counterparts to apply additional pressure on the traditional levers of domestic politics.

A new world order is emerging, with less fanfare but more substance than either the liberal internationalist or new medievalist visions. The state is not disappearing, it is disaggregating into its separate, functionally distinct parts. These parts—courts, regulatory agencies, executives, and even legislatures—are networking with their counterparts abroad, creating a dense web of relations that constitutes a new, transgovernmental order. Today's international problems—terrorism, organized crime, environmental degradation, money laundering, bank failure, and securities fraud—created and sustain these relations. Government institutions have formed networks of their own, ranging from the Basle Committee of Central Bankers to informal ties between law enforcement agencies to legal networks that make foreign judicial decisions more and more familiar. While political scientists Robert Keohane and Joseph Nye first observed its emergence in the 1970s, today transgovernmentalism is rapidly becoming the most widespread and effective mode of international governance.

Compared to the lofty ideals of liberal internationalism and the exuberant possibilities of the new medievalism, transgovernmentalism seems mundane. Meetings between securities regulators, antitrust or environmental officials, judges, or legislators lack the drama of high politics. But for the internationalists of the 1990s—bankers, lawyers, businesspeople, public-interest activists, and criminals—transnational government networks are a reality. Wall Street looks to the Basle Committee rather than the World Bank. Human rights lawyers are more likely to develop transnational litigation strategies for domestic courts than to petition the U.N. Committee on Human Rights.

Moreover, transgovernmentalism has many virtues. It is a key element of a bipartisan foreign policy, simultaneously assuaging conservative fears of a loss of sovereignty to international institutions and liberal fears of a loss of regulatory power in a globalized economy. While presidential candidate Pat Buchanan and Senator Jesse Helms (R-N.C.) demonize the U.N. and the WTO as supranational bureaucracies that seek to dictate to national governments, Senators Ted Kennedy (D-Mass.) and Paul Wellstone (D-Mich.) inveigh against international capital mobility as the catalyst of a global "race to the bottom" in regulatory standards. Networks of bureaucrats responding to international crises and planning to prevent future problems are more flexible than international institutions and expand the regulatory reach of all participating nations. This combination of flexibility and effectiveness offers something for both sides of the aisle.

Transgovernmentalism also offers promising new mechanisms for the Clinton administration's "enlargement" policy, aiming to expand the community of liberal democracies. Contrary to Samuel Huntington's gloomy predictions in The Clash of Civilizations and the New World Order (1996), existing government networks span civilizations, drawing in courts from Argentina to Zimbabwe and financial regulators from Japan to Saudi Arabia. The dominant institutions in these networks remain concentrated in North America and Western Europe, but their impact can be felt in every corner of the globe. Moreover, disaggregating the state makes it possible to assess the quality of specific judicial, administrative, and legislative institutions, whether or not the governments are liberal democracies. Regular interaction with foreign colleagues offers new channels for spreading democratic accountability, governmental integrity, and the rule of law.

An offspring of an increasingly borderless world, transgovernmentalism is a world order ideal in its own right, one that is more effective and potentially more accountable than either of the current alternatives. Liberal internationalism poses the prospect of a supranational bureaucracy answerable to no one. The new medievalist vision appeals equally to states' rights enthusiasts and supranationalists, but could easily reflect the worst of both worlds. Transgovernmentalism, by contrast, leaves the control of government institutions in the hands of national citizens, who must hold their governments as accountable for their transnational activities as for their domestic duties.

JUDICIAL FOREIGN POLICY

Judges are building a global community of law. They share values and interests based on their belief in the law as distinct but not divorced from politics and their view of themselves as professionals who must be insulated from direct political influence. At its best, this global community reminds each participant that his or her professional performance is being monitored and supported by a larger audience.

National and international judges are networking, becoming increasingly aware of one another and of their stake in a common enterprise. The most informal level of transnational judicial contact is knowledge of foreign and international judicial decisions and a corresponding willingness to cite them. The Israeli Supreme Court and the German and Canadian constitutional courts have long researched U.S. Supreme Court precedents in reaching their own conclusions on questions like freedom of speech, privacy rights, and due process. Fledgling constitutional courts in Central and Eastern Europe and in Russia are eagerly following suit. In 1995, the South African Supreme Court, finding the death penalty unconstitutional under the national constitution, referred to decisions from national and supranational courts around the world, including ones in Hungary, India, Tanzania, Canada, and Germany and the European Court of Human Rights. The U.S. Supreme Court has typically been more of a giver than a receiver in this exchange, but Justice Sandra Day O'Connor recently chided American lawyers and judges for their insularity in ignoring foreign law and predicted that she and her fellow justices would find themselves "looking more frequently to the decisions of other constitutional courts."

Why should a court in Israel or South Africa cite a decision by the U. S. Supreme Court in reaching its own conclusion? Decisions rendered by outside courts can have no authoritative value. They carry weight only because of their intrinsic logical power or because the court invoking them seeks to gain legitimacy by linking itself to a larger community of courts considering similar issues. National courts have become increasingly aware that they and their foreign counterparts are often engaged in a common effort to delimit the boundaries of individual rights in the face of an apparently overriding public interest. Thus, the British House of Lords recently rebuked the U.S. Supreme Court for its decision to uphold the kidnapping of a Mexican doctor by U.S. officials determined to bring him to trial in the United States.

Judges also cooperate in resolving transnational or international disputes. In cases involving citizens of two different states, courts have long been willing to acknowledge each other's potential interest and to defer to one another when such deference is not too costly. U.S. courts now recognize that they may become involved in a sustained dialogue with a foreign court. For instance, Judge Guido Calabresi of the Second Circuit recently allowed a French litigant to invoke U.S. discovery provisions without exhausting discovery options in France, reasoning that it was up to the French courts to identify and protest any infringements of French sovereignty. U.S. courts would then respond to such protests.

Judicial communication is not always harmonious, as in a recent squabble between a U.S. judge and a Hong Kong judge over an insider trading case. The U.S. judge refused to decline jurisdiction in favor of the Hong Kong court on grounds that "in Hong Kong they practically give you a medal for doing this sort of thing [insider trading]." In response, the Hong Kong judge stiffly defended the adequacy of Hong Kong law and asserted his willingness to apply it. He also chided his American counterpart, pointing out that any conflict "should be approached in the spirit of judicial comity rather than judicial competitiveness." Such conflict is to be expected among diplomats, but what is striking here is the two courts' view of themselves as quasi-autonomous foreign policy actors doing battle against international securities fraud.

The most advanced form of judicial cooperation is a partnership between national courts and a supranational tribunal. In the European Union (EU), the European Court of Justice works with national courts when questions of European law overlap national law. National courts refer cases up to the European Court, which issues an opinion and sends the case back to national courts; the supranational recommendation guides the national court's decision. This cooperation marshals the power of domestic courts behind the judgment of a supranational tribunal. While the Treaty of Rome provides for this reference procedure, it is the courts that have transformed it into a judicial partnership.

Finally, judges are talking face to face. The judges of the supreme courts of Western Europe began meeting every three years in 1978. Since then they have become more aware of one another's decisions, particularly with regard to each other's willingness to accept the decisions handed down by the European Court of Justice. Meetings between U.S. Supreme Court justices and their counterparts on the European Court have been sponsored by private groups, as have meetings of U.S. judges with judges from the supreme courts of Central and Eastern Europe and Russia.

The most formal initiative aimed at bringing judges together is the recently inaugurated Organization of the Supreme Courts of the Americas. Twenty-five supreme court justices or their designees met in Washington in October 1995 and drafted the OCSA charter, dedicating the organization to "promot[ing] and strengthen[ing] judicial independence and the rule of law among the members, as well as the proper constitutional treatment of the judiciary as a fundamental branch of the state." The charter calls for triennial meetings and envisages a permanent secretariat. It required ratification by 15 supreme courts, achieved in spring 1996. An initiative by judges, for judges, it is not a stretch to say that OCSA is the product of judicial foreign policy.

Champions of a global rule of law have most frequently envisioned one rule for all, a unified legal system topped by a world court. The global community of law emerging from judicial networks will more likely encompass many rules of law, each established in a specific state or region. No high court would hand down definitive global rules. National courts would interact with one another and with supranational tribunals in ways that would accommodate differences but acknowledge and reinforce common values.

THE REGULATORY WEB

The densest area of transgovernmental activity is among national regulators. Bureaucrats charged with the administration of antitrust policy, securities regulation, environmental policy, criminal law enforcement, banking and insurance supervision—in short, all the agents of the modern regulatory state—regularly collaborate with their foreign counterparts.

National regulators track their quarry through cooperation. While frequently ad hoc, such cooperation is increasingly cemented by bilateral and multilateral agreements. The most formal of these are mutual legal assistance treaties, whereby two states lay out a protocol governing cooperation between their law enforcement agencies and courts. However, the preferred instrument of cooperation is the memorandum of understanding, in which two or more regulatory agencies set forth and initial terms for an ongoing relationship. Such memorandums are not treaties; they do not engage the executive or the legislature in negotiations, deliberation, or signature. Rather, they are good-faith agreements, affirming ties between regulatory agencies based on their like-minded commitment to getting results.

"Positive comity," a concept developed by the U.S. Department of Justice, epitomizes the changing nature of transgovernmental relations. Comity of nations, an archaic and notoriously vague term beloved by diplomats and international lawyers, has traditionally signified the deference one nation grants another in recognition of their mutual sovereignty. For instance, a state will recognize another state's laws or judicial judgments based on comity. Positive comity requires more active cooperation. As worked out by the Antitrust Division of the U.S. Department of Justice and the EU's European Commission, the regulatory authorities of both states alert one another to violations within their jurisdiction, with the understanding that the responsible authority will take action. Positive comity is a principle of enduring cooperation between government agencies.

In 1988 the central bankers of the world's major financial powers adopted capital adequacy requirements for all banks under their supervision—a significant reform of the international banking system. It was not the World Bank, the International Monetary Fund, or even the Group of Seven that took this step. Rather, the forum was the Basle Committee on Banking Supervision, an organization composed of 12 central bank governors. The Basle Committee was created by a simple agreement among the governors themselves. Its members meet four times a year and follow their own rules. Decisions are made by consensus and are not formally binding; however, members do implement these decisions within their own systems. The Basle Committee's authority is often cited as an argument for taking domestic action.

National securities commissioners and insurance regulators have followed the Basle Committee's example. Incorporated by a private bill of the Quebec National Assembly, the International Organization of Securities Commissioners has no formal charter or founding treaty. Its primary purpose is to solve problems affecting international securities markets by creating a consensus for enactment of national legislation. Its members have also entered into information-sharing agreements on their own initiative. The International Association of Insurance Supervisors follows a similar model, as does the newly created Tripartite Group, an international coalition of banking, insurance, and securities regulators the Basle Committee created to improve the supervision of financial conglomerates.

Pat Buchanan would have had a field day with the Tripartite Group, denouncing it as a prime example of bureaucrats taking power out of the hands of American voters. In fact, unlike the international bogeymen of demagogic fantasy, transnational regulatory organizations do not aspire to exercise power in the international system independent of their members. Indeed, their main purpose is to help regulators apprehend those who would harm the interests of American voters. Transgovernmental networks often promulgate their own rules, but the purpose of those rules is to enhance the enforcement of national law.

Traditional international law requires states to implement the international obligations they incur through their own law. Thus, if states agree to a 12-mile territorial sea, they must change their domestic legislation concerning the interdiction of vessels in territorial waters accordingly. But this legislation is unlikely to overlap with domestic law, as national legislatures do not usually seek to regulate global commons issues and interstate relations.

Transgovernmental regulation, by contrast, produces rules concerning issues that each nation already regulates within its borders: crime, securities fraud, pollution, tax evasion. The advances in technology and transportation that have fueled globalization have made it more difficult to enforce national law. Regulators benefit from coordinating their enforcement efforts with those of their foreign counterparts and from ensuring that other nations adopt similar approaches.

The result is the nationalization of international law. Regulatory agreements between states are pledges of good faith that are self-enforcing, in the sense that each nation will be better able to enforce its national law by implementing the agreement if other nations do likewise. Laws are binding or coercive only at the national level.

Uniformity of result and diversity of means go hand in hand, and the makers and enforcers of rules are national leaders who are accountable to the people.

BIPARTISAN GLOBALIZATION

Secretary of State Madeleine Albright seeks to revive the bipartisan foreign policy consensus of the late 1940s. Deputy Secretary of State Strobe Talbott argues that promoting democracy worldwide satisfies the American need for idealpolitik as well as realpolitik. President Clinton, in his second inaugural address, called for a "new government for a new century," abroad as well as at home. But bipartisanship is threatened by divergent responses to globalization, democratization is a tricky business, and Vice President Al Gore's efforts to "reinvent government" have focused on domestic rather than international institutions. Transgovernmentalism can address all these problems.

Globalization implies the erosion of national boundaries. Consequently, regulators' power to implement national regulations within those boundaries declines both because people can easily flee their jurisdiction and because the flows of capital, pollution, pathogens, and weapons are too great and sudden for any one regulator to control. The liberal internationalist response to these assaults on state regulatory power is to build a larger international apparatus. Globalization thus leads to internationalization, or the transfer of regulatory authority from the national level to an international institution. The best example is not the WTO itself, but rather the stream of proposals to expand the WTO's jurisdiction to global competition policy, intellectual property regulation, and other trade-related issues. Liberals are likely to support expanding the power of international institutions to guard against the global dismantling of the regulatory state.

Here's the rub. Conservatives are more likely to favor the expansion of globalized markets without the internationalization that goes with it, since internationalization, from their perspective, equals a loss of sovereignty. According to Buchanan, the U.S. foreign policy establishment "want[s] to move America into a New World Order where the World Court decides quarrels between nations; the WTO writes the rules for trade and settles all disputes; the IMF and World Bank order wealth transfers from continent to continent and country to country; the Law of the Sea Treaty tells us what we may and may not do on the high seas and ocean floor, and the United Nations decides where U.S. military forces may and may not intervene." The rhetoric is deliberately inflammatory, but echoes resound across the Republican spectrum.

Transgovernmental initiatives are a compromise that could command bipartisan support. Regulatory loopholes caused by global forces require a coordinated response beyond the reach of any one country. But this coordination need not come from building more international institutions. It can be achieved through transgovernmental cooperation, involving the same officials who make and implement policy at the national level. The transgovernmental alternative is fast, flexible, and effective.

A leading example of transgovernmentalism in action that demonstrates its bipartisan appeal is a State Department initiative christened the New Transatlantic Agenda. Launched in 1991 under the Bush administration and reinvigorated by Secretary of State Warren Christopher in 1995, the initiative structures the relationship between the United States and the EU, fostering cooperation in areas ranging from opening markets to fighting terrorism, drug trafficking, and infectious disease. It is an umbrella for ongoing projects between U.S. officials and their European counterparts. It reaches ordinary citizens, embracing efforts like the Transatlantic Business Dialogue and engaging individuals through people-to-people exchanges and expanded communication through the Internet.

DEMOCRATIZATION, STEP BY STEP

Transgovernmental networks are concentrated among liberal democracies but are not limited to them. Some nondemocratic states have institutions capable of cooperating with their foreign counterparts, such as committed and effective regulatory agencies or relatively independent judiciaries. Transgovernmental ties can strengthen institutions in ways that will help them resist political domination, corruption, and incompetence and build democratic institutions in their countries, step by step. The Organization of Supreme Courts of the Americas, for instance, actively seeks to strengthen norms of judicial independence among its members, many of whom must fend off powerful political forces.

Individuals and groups in nondemocratic countries may also "borrow" government institutions of democratic states to achieve a measure of justice they cannot obtain in their own countries. The court or regulatory agency of one state may be able to perform judicial or regulatory functions for the people of another. Victims of human rights violations, for example, in countries such as Argentina, Ethiopia, Haiti, and the Philippines have sued for redress in the courts of the United States. U.S. courts accepted these cases, often over the objections of the executive branch, using a broad interpretation of a moribund statute dating back to 1789. Under this interpretation, aliens may sue in U.S. courts to seek damages from foreign government officials accused of torture, even if the torture allegedly took place in the foreign country. More generally, a nongovernmental organization seeking to prevent human rights violations can often circumvent their own government's corrupt legislature and politicized court by publicizing the plight of victims abroad and mobilizing a foreign court, legislature, or executive to take action.

Responding to calls for a coherent U.S. foreign policy and seeking to strengthen the community of democratic nations, President Clinton substituted the concept of "enlargement" for the Cold War principle of "containment." Expanding transgovernmental outreach to include institutions from nondemocratic states would help expand the circle of democracies one institution at a time.

A NEW WORLD ORDER IDEAL

Transgovernmentalism offers its own world order ideal, less dramatic but more compelling than either liberal internationalism or the new medievalism. It harnesses the state's power to find and implement solutions to global problems. International institutions have a lackluster record on such problem-solving; indeed, ngos exist largely to compensate for their inadequacies. Doing away with the state, however, is hardly the answer. The new medievalist mantra of global governance is "governance without government." But governance without government is governance without power, and government without power rarely works. Many pressing international and domestic problems result from states' insufficient power to establish order, build infrastructure, and provide minimum social services. Private actors may take up some slack, but there is no substitute for the state.

Transgovernmental networks allow governments to benefit from the flexibility and decentralization of nonstate actors. Jessica T. Mathews argues that "businesses, citizens' organizations, ethnic groups, and crime cartels have all readily adopted the network model," while governments "are quintessential hierarchies, wedded to an organizational form incompatible with all that the new technologies make possible." Not so. Disaggregating the state into its functional components makes it possible to create networks of institutions engaged in a common enterprise even as they represent distinct national interests. Moreover, they can work with their subnational and supranational counterparts, creating a genuinely new world order in which networked institutions perform the functions of a world government—legislation, administration, and adjudication—without the form.

These globe-spanning networks will strengthen the state as the primary player in the international system. The state's defining attribute has traditionally been sovereignty, conceived as absolute power in domestic affairs and autonomy in relations with other states. But as Abram and Antonia Chayes observe in The New Sovereignty (1995), sovereignty is actually "status—the vindication of the state's existence in the international system." More importantly, they demonstrate that in contemporary international relations, sovereignty has been redefined to mean "membership ... in the regimes that make up the substance of international life." Disaggregating the state permits the disaggregation of sovereignty as well, ensuring that specific state institutions derive strength and status from participation in a transgovernmental order.

Transgovernmental networks will increasingly provide an important anchor for international organizations and nonstate actors alike. U.N. officials have already learned a lesson about the limits of supranational authority; mandated cuts in the international bureaucracy will further tip the balance of power toward national regulators. The next generation of international institutions is also likely to look more like the Basle Committee, or, more formally, the Organization of Economic Cooperation and Development, dedicated to providing a forum for transnational problem-solving and the harmonization of national law. The disaggregation of the state creates opportunities for domestic institutions, particularly courts, to make common cause with their supranational counterparts against their fellow branches of government. Nonstate actors will lobby and litigate wherever they think they will have the most effect. Many already realize that corporate self-regulation and states' promises to comply with vague international agreements are no substitute for national law.

The spread of transgovernmental networks will depend more on political and professional convergence than on civilizational boundaries. Trust and awareness of a common enterprise are more vulnerable to differing political ideologies and corruption than to cultural differences. Government networks transcend the traditional divide between high and low politics. National militaries, for instance, network as extensively as central bankers with their counterparts in friendly states. Judicial and regulatory networks can help achieve gradual political convergence, but are unlikely to be of much help in the face of a serious economic or military threat. If the coming conflict with China is indeed coming, transgovernmentalism will not stop it.

The strength of transgovernmental networks and of transgovernmentalism as a world order ideal will ultimately depend on their accountability to the world's peoples. To many, the prospect of transnational government by judges and bureaucrats looks more like technocracy than democracy. Critics contend that government institutions engaged in policy coordination with their foreign counterparts will be barely visible, much less accountable, to voters still largely tied to national territory.

Citizens of liberal democracies will not accept any form of international regulation they cannot control. But checking unelected officials is a familiar problem in domestic politics. As national legislators become increasingly aware of transgovernmental networks, they will expand their oversight capacities and develop networks of their own. Transnational NGO networks will develop a similar monitoring capacity. It will be harder to monitor themselves.

Transgovernmentalism offers answers to the most important challenges facing advanced industrial countries: loss of regulatory power with economic globalization, perceptions of a "democratic deficit" as international institutions step in to fill the regulatory gap, and the difficulties of engaging nondemocratic states. Moreover, it provides a powerful alternative to a liberal internationalism that has reached its limits and to a new medievalism that, like the old Marxism, sees the state slowly fading away. The new medievalists are right to emphasize the dawn of a new era, in which information technology will transform the globe. But government networks are government for the information age. They offer the world a blueprint for the international architecture of the 21st century.

Anne-Marie Slaughter is the J. Sinclair Armstrong Professor of International, Foreign, and Comparative Law at Harvard Law School.

Globalization and Its Discontents: Navigating the Dangers of a Tangled World

Richard N. Haass and Robert Litan

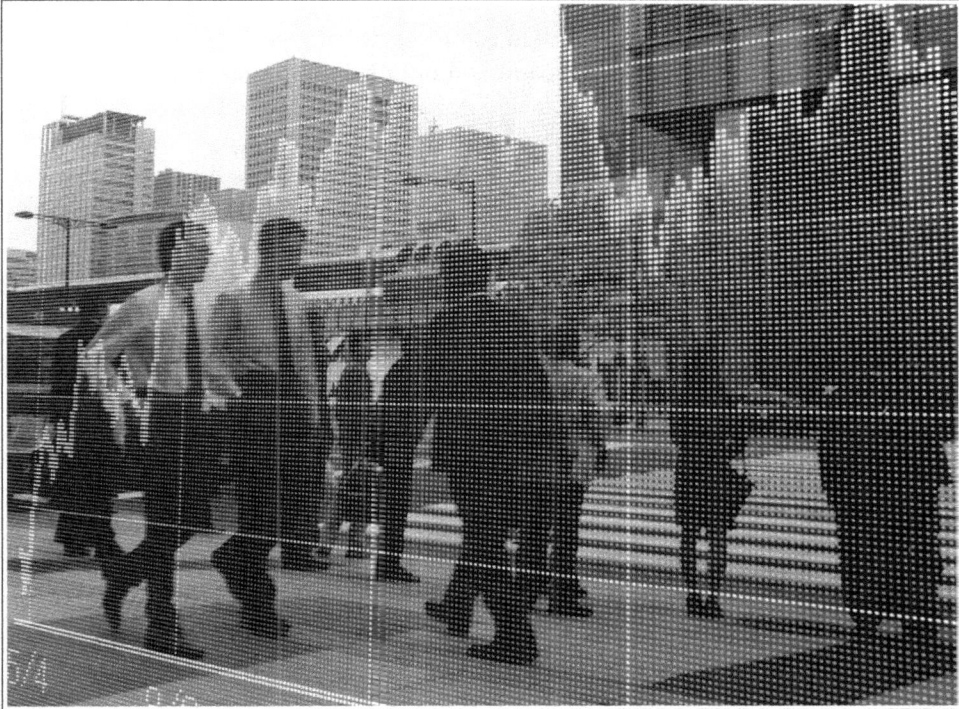

The period immediately following the Second World War, which produced the Marshall Plan, NATO, and the U.S.-Japan security treaty, is rightly regarded as foreign policy's golden era. But it also saw the birth of comparably successful economic institutions— such as the International Monetary Fund, the World Bank, the General Agreement on Tariffs and Trade—designed to promote long-term prosperity through stable exchange rates, worldwide development, and open trade. Today these institutions are increasingly subject to criticism. The IMF, for instance, has come under attack for imposing drastic conditions in its "rescues" of Mexico in 1995 and Asia today. The World Trade Organization, formed in 1995 as the result of American calls for a body to resolve market-access disputes, has been attacked in this country for usurping America's sovereignty. And doubts abound about the role of development banks in an era of massive direct foreign investment.

The gap between the legacy of Bretton Woods and the economic and political demands of the modern world is growing. Much of this change is driven by rapid advances in, and thus lower costs of, communications, information flows, and travel. Official policy, much of it American, has played its part by reducing barriers to the movement of goods and capital across national boundaries. The result has been more intrusive and intense economic interaction—including the explosive growth of world capital markets, which led to the demise of fixed exchange rates—between a large and growing number of entities outside government control, a phenomenon that has come to be called "globalization."

But globalization has its problems. In some quarters it is seen as having caused the rapid flows of investment that moved in and out of countries as investor sentiment changed and were behind the Mexican and Asian financial crises. In the United States it is blamed for job losses, increasing income inequality, and stagnant or deteriorating real wages. Domestic discontent with globalization thwarted the passage last year of legislation that would have granted the president "fast track" authority to negotiate trade arrangements that Congress could not modify.

Globalization has become a target. Its dangers must be navigated successfully or the United States and others may be compelled to backtrack, diminishing the free movement of goods, services, and capital, which would result in slower growth, less technological innovation, and lower living standards.

FREE-MARKET FOREIGN POLICY?

In this new world, poor economic policymaking, corrupt banking practices, dishonest accounting, and unrealistic currency alignments can have an impact on societies far removed. Although the United States, with its vast internal market, is considerably less "globalized" than other industrialized countries, millions of American jobs and billions of dollars are tied to economic developments elsewhere.

If there is consensus on the diagnosis, there is none on the prescription. There are at least three fundamentally different approaches to addressing the problems of the global economy.

The first embraces the free market and would abandon IMF-like rescue packages. It is motivated by the belief that the IMF lulls governments, investors, and lenders into recklessness. Emboldened by the prospect that the IMF will come to their rescue, they are free to act irresponsibly. In the words of George Shultz, William Simon, and Walter Wriston, IMF "interference will only encourage more crises." Mexico, in this view, led to Asia.

The laissez-faire, free-market approach looks good in the abstract because markets reward sound investments and regulatory practices and punish poor ones. In principle, it can provide incentives for investors to avoid overly risky investments and for governments to adopt prudent policies. To international free marketeers, safety nets destroy this incentive.

But this critique goes too far. Governments submitting to IMF rescue plans must often agree to wrenching reforms—not the kind of experience that invites other governments to be reckless. Similarly, investors in equity markets in Mexico and Asia were hit by depressed local stock prices and heavily devalued local currencies. The only parties that emerged relatively unscathed, and thus for whom the free market critique has some relevance, were certain creditors: holders of Mexican government debt during the Mexican crisis and banks in the recent Asian crisis.

The solution to this problem is not to remove the IMF—the international lender of last resort—but to develop ways to warn banks and other creditors that they will suffer in the event of a future crisis. During the Depression, Americans learned the cost of not having a functioning lender of last resort: a wave of bank and corporate failures, aggravated by a shortage of liquidity that the Federal Reserve failed to provide. The international equivalent of having no Fed is standing idly by while currencies plummet, countries run out of foreign exchange, trade and investment come to a halt, and crises in one region spread to others.

A hands-off approach would risk transforming limited crises into something much more costly. More than economics is at stake. Years of punishment by the marketplace are simply not acceptable when immediate strategic interests are involved, as they are, for example, in Mexico or South Korea. For better or worse, the United States cannot afford the collapse of countries vital to its national interest.

GOVERNING GLOBALIZATION

The second approach to taming the dangers of globalization could hardly be more different. It suggests the creation of new institutions to lend structure and direction to the global marketplace, complementing what is seen as the constructive but inadequate roles of the IMF and other bodies. For example, George Soros, arguing that "international capital movements need to be supervised and the allocation of credit regulated," has recommended creating the international equivalent of the United States' Fannie Mae, which guarantees residential mortgages for a fee. He calls for the establishment of an "International Credit Insurance Corporation" that would guarantee private sector loans up to a specified amount for a modest charge, while requiring that the borrowers' home countries provide a complete financial picture in order for them to qualify.

Henry Kaufman, a Wall Street economist, would go even further, creating a "Board of Overseers of Major International Institutions and Markets" that would set minimum capital requirements for all institutions, establish uniform accounting and lending standards, and monitor performance. It would even discipline those who did not meet these criteria by limiting the ability of those who remained outside the system to lend, borrow, and sell.

Governments are sure to resist supranational bodies that so fundamentally challenge their sovereignty. Moreover, except for extreme crises when an IMF-like rescue is warranted, it is difficult to understand why international officials could determine how much credit to allocate better than the market. There is more than a little irony in applying the "Asian model" of centralization to the international economy just when the model has been so thoroughly discredited.

A third approach, which would leave the basic architecture of the international economy alone but still do some "remodeling," would involve a number of reforms designed to structure and discipline financial operations and transactions. This managed approach would eschew the heavy hand of international regulation but aim to maintain the element of risk essential to capitalism without removing the safety net provided by the IMF. This approach is closest to the manner in which the United States dealt with the savings and loan and banking crises of the 1980s: enacting legislation requiring shareholders to maintain a larger financial commitment to their banks while making it more difficult for regulators and policymakers to bail out large, uninsured depositors who could previously count on being protected. The challenge for the international community is to introduce the equivalent of the U.S. reforms at both the national and international levels.

Such reforms are already being worked on at the behest of the IMF. They include improving the supervision of financial institutions, instituting Western-style accounting practices in banks and corporations, and opening up markets to foreign investment. To ensure that these reforms are carried out, some other international body, such as the Bank for International Settlements or perhaps a nongovernmental organization, should issue regular "report cards" on individual countries' progress. In addition, the IMF must press countries to be forthcoming with accurate information about key financial data, including their current account positions, foreign exchange reserves, and short-term indebtedness to foreign creditors. Banks and investors will favor countries that are positively rated, and penalize or avoid those that are not. Governments and institutions will introduce desirable reforms lest they lose out.

More transparency and information is necessary but not sufficient for markets to avoid excesses. The challenge is to find effective ways of addressing the free market critique. A possible solution is for the IMF to condition its assistance on countries' penalizing all lenders of foreign currency in the event IMF intervention is required. In particular, the model legislation that each country could adopt would require (as long as an IMF rescue is in effect) that creditors automatically suffer some loss of their principal when their debt matures and is not rolled over or extended. This approach would discourage the sudden outflow of maturing debt when countries can least afford it. The threat of automatic loss in the event a country experiences economic crisis could underscore to banks and other creditors that their money is at risk and that they can no longer count on the IMF to bail them out. Creditors would respond, of course, by insisting on higher interest rates for borrowers with opaque or poorly capitalized balance sheets. But that is precisely the point: the price of loans should better reflect the risk of not getting repaid.

The Asian crisis demonstrates the need for more formal bankruptcy codes and mechanisms for restructuring the balance sheets of heavily indebted firms without necessarily shutting them down. Existing international institutions can assist countries in this area, as well as in strengthening bank supervision and accounting standards, but there is no need to establish a new international bankruptcy court or to vest existing international institutions with such powers. The United States has a bankruptcy code and process that handles insolvency of firms located here, even when they have foreign creditors. There is no reason why other countries cannot do the same thing.

THE HOME FRONT

To paraphrase former House Speaker Tip O'Neill, all economics is local. Policies promoting unfettered trade and investment will be rejected by Congress unless steps are taken to build a firm domestic political base. Once again, there are three approaches to choose from, running the gamut from laissez faire to heavy regulation. A pure market approach—one that would let the chips (and the workers) fall where they may—would be neither fair nor politically sustainable. Some sort of safety net is both desirable and necessary. At the same time, it would be foolish to try to insulate Americans from all of globalization's effects. It is impossible to protect jobs rendered obsolete by technological change and foreign competition. What lies between is a managed approach that helps workers cope with the consequences of globalization. It would both change and supplement existing programs and policies.

Since 1962, American policymakers have provided extended unemployment insurance to workers who can prove they were displaced primarily because of international trade. But this discourages workers from looking for employment, channeling them toward government training programs with little proven success. Moreover, it does not compensate workers for the cuts in pay they take even after finding new jobs. A more effective program would pay workers a portion of the difference between their wages at their previous and new jobs. This kind of earnings insurance would encourage workers to take new jobs even if they paid less, and offer the only real training that works—on the job. Workers could also be provided with benefits—health insurance, pensions, training, and unemployment insurance—that they could take with them when moving to a new employer.

Some will argue that portable benefits and earnings insurance are not enough. But globalization is a reality, not a choice. "You can run but you can't hide" might serve as the mantra for the age.

Those who urge us to hide by resurrecting barriers to trade and investment, with the ostensible aim of insulating Americans from the forces of globalization, would abandon America's commitment to the spread of markets and democracy around the world at precisely the moment these ideas are ascendant. Moreover, the potential economic and political cost would be enormous, depriving Americans of cheaper and in some cases higher quality goods and services, as well as denying them the opportunity to work at better paying jobs that depend on exports.

The real choice for governments is not how best to fight globalization but how to manage it, which will require creative policies both at home and abroad. It is ironic: the age of globalization may well be defined in part by challenges to the nation-state, but it is still states and governments—by the practices they adopt, the arrangements they enter into, and the safety nets they provide—that will determine whether we exploit or squander the potential of this era.

Richard N. Haass, Director of the Program in Foreign Policy Studies at the Brookings Institution, is the author of "The Reluctant Sheriff: The United States after the Cold War." Robert E. Litan, Director of Brookings' Program in Economic Studies, is co-author of "Globaphobia: Confronting Fears about Open Trade."

© Foreign Affairs

NATO at Fifty: An Unhappy Successful Marriage: Security Means Knowing What to Expect

Michael Howard

NATO was always intended to be both more and less than a military alliance. The original idea was the brainchild of Britain's foreign secretary, Ernest Bevin. In January 1948, confronted by a Western Europe still in ruins and a Soviet Union triumphantly consolidating its conquests, Bevin suggested to Washington that it would be possible to stem the further encroachment of the Soviet tide only "by organizing and consolidating the ethical and spiritual forces of Western civilization." Peace and safety, he maintained, could only be preserved by the mobilization of such moral and material force as would create confidence and energy on the one side and inspire respect and caution on the other. The alternative was to acquiesce in continued Russian infiltration and watch the piecemeal collapse of one Western bastion after another.

Cynics may allege that this downplaying of material and emphasis upon ethical force was deliberately tailored to the susceptibilities of isolationist members of Congress, but at that time the threat from the Soviet Union was not perceived primarily in military terms. The real danger seemed to lie in the moral and material exhaustion of a Western Europe that, in spite of Marshall Plan aid, still looked like a pushover for communist infiltration and propaganda. A purely military alliance did not seem the appropriate answer, but what did?

States are cold monsters that mate for convenience and self-protection, not love, and this became very clear during the negotiations for the creation of the alliance that dragged on throughout 1948. The State Department, both conscious of a Congress still hostile to any further "entangling alliances" and anxious not to accept the division of Germany and Europe as final, was at first prepared to act as no more than a benevolent godfather to a West European alliance. The French, on the other hand, remembering the desertion by their former allies in the aftermath of World War I, were demanding immediate military aid, to protect them as much against a German revival as against any Soviet threat. Canada, whose peoples were as reluctant as their neighbors to the south to become involved in any more foreign quarrels, constantly emphasized the economic and social purposes of the NATO treaty. Given the reluctance both of Canada and of the United States to enter into any specific military obligations, the final text might have lacked any military core at all if the Soviets had not helped matters along, first by mounting the communist coup in Prague in February 1948 and then by imposing the Berlin blockade in June. The impact of these events on public opinion on both sides of the Atlantic was enough to ensure the inclusion in the final text of the treaty of the famous Article 5, whereby the signatories agreed "that an armed attack against one or more of them in Europe or North America [should] be considered an attack against them all; and [that each member of the alliance would] assist the Party or Parties so attacked by taking forthwith … such action as it deems necessary, including the use of armed force, to restore and maintain international security."

Imprecise though it was, this clause provided the reassurance the Europeans wanted; but in Washington and Ottawa it was Article 2 that had the greater resonance, whereby the signatories pledged themselves to "contribute towards the further development of peaceful and friendly international relations by strengthening their free institutions, by bringing about a better understanding of the principles upon which these institutions are founded, and by promoting conditions of stability and well-being. They [undertook to] seek to eliminate conflict in their international economic policies and [to] encourage economic collaboration between any and all of them." With this bland assurance of mutual goodwill, matters might have rested but for the outbreak of the Korean War a year later in 1950, an event that was seen in Washington as the first shot in an overt Soviet bid for global expansion.

At once the aspirations expressed in Article 2 were eclipsed by the demands of Article 5—the mobilization of military forces, and the creation of a military infrastructure, to make possible a credible defense of Western Europe against an adversary that already enjoyed a crushing superiority in conventional weaponry and was already showing an alarming capacity to compete in the nuclear field.

This involved the re-creation of the wartime "Grand Alliance," this time without the Soviet Union. The British were delighted. Although the expenditure involved was to wreck their barely convalescent economy, they found themselves back where they felt they belonged: if not quite the equals of the United States, then their adjutants and mentors; certainly in a different class from the continental neighbors they had either conquered or liberated. The French had more mixed feelings. Although they welcomed the immediate influx of military aid from the United States, they resented the reassertion of a de facto Anglo-American hegemony, and—like their Benelux and Scandinavian partners—strongly objected to the price the Americans now exacted for their protection: the integration into the alliance of a West Germany without whose territory, resources, and manpower Europe would be indefensible, but whose occupation of French soil was still fresh in their memories. The price they in their turn exacted—American support for their attempt to reconquer Indochina—was to prove in the long run disastrous. As for the Germans, although the lure of American protection and the rewards that went with it was irresistible, there was understandable support for the attempt by Kurt Schumacher and the Social Democrats to find a nonaligned solution that would preserve the unity of their country and preserve them from a nuclear war being fought over their own territory. A popular cartoon at the time showed Germany as a battered little boy in a nursery where his older companions were happily re-equipping themselves with toy guns and swords, plaintively asking, "Bitte, darf ich diesmal nicht mitspielen?" ("Please, do you mind if I don't play this time?").

But how was Europe to be defended, with or without nuclear weapons? At first the solution appeared simple: the Europeans, with substantial American stiffening and under overall American command, would provide a conventional "shield," while the nuclear "sword" of the U.S. Strategic Air Command struck devastating blows deep inside the Soviet Union. When it became clear that the European allies, even with the addition of the West Germans, would be quite incapable of meeting the force levels demanded of them if their economies were ever to recover, the emphasis shifted. "Conventional" defense was downgraded to the status of a "tripwire," a burglar alarm that would still trigger an instant and overwhelming nuclear response. This, it was hoped, would "deter" a Soviet attack. But would it? During the 1950s the Soviets not only caught up with the United States in the production of thermonuclear weapons but developed the capacity, albeit one hugely overestimated by the West, to deliver them across the Atlantic. Under these circumstances was the American "nuclear guarantee" still credible, and if not, what could be done to make it so? For the next 30 years strategic thinkers on both sides of the Atlantic racked their brains in search of an answer. They never really found one.

BONES OF CONTENTION

Throughout the 1950s this nuclear dilemma was increasingly complicated by political tensions. First, whatever doubts strategic analysts may have felt about the credibility of the American military guarantee, the peoples of Western Europe felt sufficiently secure to develop thriving economies, laying the foundations for an economic community that bade fair to rival that of the United States. To some Americans this seemed, as it still seems, to be a solution rather than a problem. For President Kennedy, in one of those ill-fated "Grand Designs" that geopolitical architects in Washington were to churn out over the next four decades, European unity should be encouraged so as to provide a "second pillar" of an "Atlantic Community."

But the Europeans proved uncooperative. The Germans under Chancellor Konrad Adenauer were helpful enough, so long as their allies pledged themselves to a reunification of Germany in which none of them believed and which most of them dreaded. The British, however, still kept their distance from their continental neighbors and insisted on preserving their nuclear autonomy. As for the French, their resentment at the Anglo-Americans was brought to boiling point by the Suez crisis in 1956 and by what they saw as betrayal by their allies over their attempts to retain control in Indochina and Algeria. Under President Charles de Gaulle they began to chart their own agenda: nuclear independence, an arm's-length relationship with the alliance, a "special relationship" with the Germans, and transformation of the European Economic Community into a close political consortium dominated by Paris. To make matters worse, as the Europeans became more prosperous so their defense industries began to revive and they no longer went shopping for arms in the United States. Grumbling tensions began over "burden-sharing" that would not go away.

Second, the death of Stalin in 1953, and the more amenable attitude of his successors, were to provide another source of division within the alliance. In the view of Washington the softer winds now blowing from Moscow were the result of the staunch attitude adopted by the West, which should not in consequence be relaxed: the Soviets had simply changed their tactics in a conflict that was global, continuing, and ineluctable. The Europeans saw things differently. There political forces on the left, which everywhere remained influential even where they did not actually hold power, were always inclined to give the Soviets the benefit of any doubt, even though the brutal suppression of the Hungarian uprising in 1956 shattered the unity of all European communist parties. Domestic pressure for "detente" became a permanent feature of the European scene. This was particularly true in West Germany, where demands grew for an accommodation with the Soviet Union that would make possible the reestablishment of human contacts with fellow Germans—in many cases close relations—behind the Iron Curtain. But even such right-wing governments as those of Harold Macmillan in Britain and de Gaulle in France tended to take a traditional view of the Soviet Union, seeing it not as a permanent and implacable foe but as a great power with which they had had their difficulties in the past but with which they had been allied in two great wars; one that had interests that should be respected, but with which an accommodation was both desirable and possible. It was an attitude that Washington found very difficult to assimilate until Henry Kissinger himself adopted it a decade or so later. Increasingly, European governments had to explain to their electorates that defense, with all its associated expenditure, existed primarily to serve the purposes of detente. After a decade of increasing acrimony this was made official policy for the alliance by the Harmel Report of 1967.

Finally, divisions were growing between the allies over the geographical scope of the alliance. Ironically, in light of events in the 1990s, it was the United States that had been most insistent on limiting it to the territory of North America, Europe, and the Atlantic approaches. America had no intention of underwriting European colonial rule elsewhere in the world, and consented only with deep reluctance to include even "the Algerian departments of France" within the alliance's scope. But a decade later Washington was having second thoughts. The abandonment of European colonial rule throughout the world seemed to leave a vacuum of power into which the United States feared that the Soviet Union would feel itself free to expand, and Nikita Khrushchev's explicit support for "wars of national liberation" suggested that it intended to do so. Blocked in Europe, Soviet power appeared to be extending dangerously everywhere else. What, Washington demanded, did the Europeans intend to do about it?

The answer was, not very much. The British felt that they were discharging their obligations by doing their best to ensure a peaceful transition to independence within their own imperial possessions, especially Malaysia. The French, having painfully extricated themselves from Algeria, imposed an effective control over the rest of the Union Francaise, and felt that they had no reason to help out the Americans who had been so reluctant to assist them in their own hour of need. In any case, both British and French were skeptical of the capacity of the Soviet Union to affect the course of events in what was now called the "Third World" for good or ill, and feared that American attempts to counter it, whether in Latin America or Southeast Asia, were likely only to make matters worse. As for the Germans, they were mainly concerned lest the United States become distracted from the only issue that to them really mattered, the deterrence of Soviet aggression in Europe—a view shared by all the smaller European powers. So when the United States became engaged in Vietnam it had to soldier on alone, and did not like it.

TRIAL BY CRISIS

Deterrence, detente, burden-sharing, and "out of area"; these four issues surfaced again and again throughout the troubled history of the alliance, and would not go away. Hardly a year was to pass in which one or more of them did not cause acrimony at meetings of the NATO Council—sometimes, indeed, all four. But there were two periods when these simmering tensions seemed to reach boiling point: 1958-63, and again 20 years later, 1979-84.

In both cases the cause was the same: a sudden upsurge of doubt on the part of the United States as to whether its military deterrent posture was still credible. In 1958 this was set off by the realization that the Soviets possessed not only thermonuclear weapons, but a capacity to deliver them onto American soil. The flight of the manned satellite Sputnik in 1957 indicated indeed that Soviet space technology might be even more advanced than that of the United States, where fears of a "missile gap" grew almost to panic proportions. In 1958 Khrushchev exploited this in an attempt to heal his own chief source of vulnerability, the hemorrhage of East Germans fleeing from communist rule through Berlin; first by demanding the termination of four-power rights over the city, then in 1961 by consenting to the erection of the Berlin Wall. The peoples of Europe suddenly saw themselves confronted by the alternatives of a bloodless Soviet victory and a suicidal nuclear war, and a cry went up for nuclear disarmament and disengagement from the United States. The crisis came to a head over Cuba in 1962 and was weathered by a firm American leadership that did much to restore European confidence. The Americans themselves were reassured by the discovery that their original fears had been largely groundless, but they initiated, under Secretary of Defense Robert McNamara, a major armament program to ensure that no such perceptions of vulnerability should arise again.

The Europeans remained deeply unsettled by the experience. Both the British and the French were reinforced in their determination to retain their own nuclear reinsurance systems. Fears that the Germans might wish to follow their example led the United States to propose the construction of a Multilateral Nuclear Force—a project that merely evoked universal mockery and was deservedly rejected. In fact the Germans were far more seriously concerned by McNamara's attempt to create a more credible deterrent posture with his doctrine of "flexible response." On whose territory, asked the Germans with good reason, did the Americans intend to be flexible? In general the crisis left both sides badly bruised. The Europeans resented the patronizing didacticism of McNamara's brilliant young strategic analysts, while the Americans were exasperated by the constant European demands for reassurance from their protectors without doing anything to make that reassurance realistic. Kissinger was to voice American frustrations but again to reawaken European fears when in 1979, under very similar strategic circumstances, he told a conference celebrating NATO's 30th anniversary that "our European allies should not keep asking us to multiply strategic assurances that we cannot possibly mean, or if we did mean, we should not want to execute because if we execute, we risk the destruction of civilization."

The tensions within the alliance relaxed somewhat over the next 15 years. The United States entered into arms control negotiations that did something to draw the sting of the European left. Washington's attention was diverted to "out of area" problems, first Vietnam, then the Middle East, in the resolution of which Kissinger tended to treat the Soviet Union almost as a colleague rather than an adversary. But these distractions created their own difficulties. Bilateral negotiations over arms control were complicated by the fears and interests of the European allies, who voiced alternately complaints about the talks' lack of progress and fears that the superpowers were reaching agreements that ignored Europeans' own security interests. Over Vietnam, as we have seen, the Americans intensely resented the lack of European support, while the Europeans observed with alarm the apparent degradation of U.S. forces in Europe and the growing demands in Congress for yet further American troop withdrawals.

As for the Middle East and the crisis that arose there in 1973 over the Yom Kippur War, Americans with their pro-Israeli sympathies and Europeans dependent on Arab-controlled oil found themselves virtually on opposing sides. Doing nothing to help were the facts that in Britain, for the first time since the war, a government was in power, under Edward Heath, that rated good relations with its European neighbors more highly than the "special relationship" with the United States; that in Germany a Social Democratic government had come into office pursuing an independent Ostpolitik; and that the French remained predictably unhelpful under de Gaulle's designated successor, President Georges Pompidou. Kissinger's ill-judged and patronizing attempt to soothe European susceptibilities by declaring 1973 to be the "Year of Europe" only made matters worse.

After that relations improved, though ill-tempered arguments about burden-sharing and support costs grumbled on at lower levels of the alliance bureaucracy. In 1974 an emollient "Atlantic Declaration" was issued reassuring the allies that they were all on the same side. In Britain a Labour government had been returned to power whose mismanagement of the national economy made it more dependent than ever on American goodwill. More pragmatic administrations came into power in France under Valery Giscard d'Estaing and Francois Mitterrand. As for the Germans, their Ostpolitik initiative, at first viewed in Washington with extreme mistrust, had resulted in the settlement of central European frontiers over which wars had been fought for generations, and had ripened into the Helsinki conferences that were gradually to transform relations between Eastern and Western Europe, if not with the Soviet Union itself. By the end of the decade the European weather at last seemed set fair— which made the onset of the crisis years, 1979-84, all the more traumatic.

This new period of tension was precipitated, like the first, by a crisis in American self-confidence. The steady buildup of the Soviet military arsenal throughout the 1970s, including the modernization of nuclear weapons targeted on Western Europe, had caused concern on both sides of the Atlantic, and members of the alliance agreed to increase their defense expenditures to deal with it. In American eyes this buildup appeared all the more sinister in light of increasingly bold Soviet interventions in southern and eastern Africa, the dreadful humiliations suffered by the United States in the course of the Iranian Revolution, and worst of all, the Soviet invasion of Afghanistan in December 1979. The apparent lack of interest by their European allies in these developments enraged the Americans, as did the insouciance with which the Europeans continued to exploit the opening trade opportunities with the Soviet Union and Eastern Europe. The incoming Reagan administration treated its allies with a brusqueness bordering on brutality that infuriated their governments, and adopted toward the Soviets a posture of rhetorical hostility that alarmed their peoples.

Once again the fear of imminent nuclear war (felt as strongly this time in Moscow as anywhere else) created political turmoil in Europe. In spite of their other differences with Washington, European governments recognized the strategic necessity of accepting the installation of American missiles to counter the Soviet SS-20s aimed at their own territory, but they had huge difficulty in persuading their own peoples to do the same. Hardly had this crisis been resolved than a further problem was created by President Reagan's unilateral proclamation of a Strategic Defense Initiative that seemed likely to destroy all hope of serious arms control agreements, appeared to undermine the entire strategic doctrine on which the alliance was based, and made even America's friends fear a return to a doctrine of "Fortress America." To many in Europe, Reagan seemed a greater threat to peace than did the geriatric leadership of the Soviet Union, while it was widely believed in the United States that the Europeans had been cowed by Soviet strength into a servile condition of "Finlandization."

Then suddenly it all ended. Like Kennedy before him, President Reagan had mastered the crisis, not only by a massive arms buildup that restored self-confidence (while wrecking the economy) of the United States, but also by maintaining contact, in spite of all his rhetoric, with the Soviet leadership. In 1985 there emerged a leader, Mikhail Gorbachev, that he could do business with, and Reagan, to his eternal credit, seized the opportunity. Within six years the Cold War was at an end, Germany was reunited, the Warsaw Pact had dissolved, and Soviet troops were withdrawing to their own frontiers.

ITS FINEST HOUR

Historians will long debate whether the collapse of the Soviet Union owed more to the unremitting pressure of American arms buildups that forced it to spend itself into bankruptcy, or to the gentle but irresistible growth of popular expectations behind the Iron Curtain as the detente by which the Europeans set so much store gradually took effect; much as George Kennan had predicted it would a generation earlier. But what is beyond doubt is that the alliance never worked so effectively in conducting the Cold War as it did in bringing it to an end.

Had Gorbachev been less complaisant matters might have been different. As it was, the excellent rapport established between the American and Soviet leaderships was complemented by that between a German chancellor, Helmut Kohl, who knew exactly what he wanted—German unification—and an American president who firmly supported him in spite of the doubts of his other alliance partners. The French under President Mitterrand were unwontedly cooperative: whatever their feelings about the Americans, they dared not antagonize a Germany whose friendship was essential in creating an effective European Union. The British under Prime Minister Margaret Thatcher were initially reluctant; but whatever their feelings about Germany, they did not dare do anything to upset the "special relationship" with the United States that had paid such excellent dividends in helping Britain recover the Falkland Islands from Argentina in 1982. The treaty signed in Paris in November 1990 not only brought the Cold War to an end but established a new structure of international relations among scenes of international amity barely witnessed since the Congress of Vienna in 1815.

Now we celebrate the Golden Anniversary of a highly successful marriage. A successful marriage, be it noted: not a happy one. As with the arranged marriages of earlier centuries, it was entered into with a specific purpose. Such marriages had been intended to unite properties, appease enmities, and, above all, produce and bring up children. Whatever the spouses felt about each other, they stuck together to achieve these ends. The alliance had been created, in Lord Ismay's famous words, "to keep the Americans in, the Russians out, and ..." (to tactfully paraphrase his undiplomatic words) to solve the German problem. All this had happened. It had not been an easy ride. The Europeans had repeatedly found the Americans overbearing, self-righteous, and hysterically alarmist. The Americans often regarded the Europeans as a "soft" (a peculiarly American term of abuse), short-sighted, mean, and self-centered bunch of freeloaders. Familiarity made possible a modus vivendi, but bred no great affection. But the marriage worked, and the more problems it overcame, the stronger were the bonds that bound it together.

IN PRAISE OF CONTINUING

Now that the object has been achieved, voices are being raised suggesting that the marriage should be dissolved and its partners left free to look elsewhere for their security. But another characteristic of arranged marriages was that they did not dissolve even after the children had grown up. For one thing, a household had been created that remained the family home. For another, the spouses had grown used to one another, and even if there was still little affection, they had learned to make allowances for each other's infirmities. For a third, they could think of no other arrangement that was equally convenient to both. Most important of all, a separation was likely to have serious repercussions for their extended families and the society that surrounded them.

So it is with NATO. It has built up a politico-military infrastructure that integrates the armed forces of much of Europe and provides the United States with a unique capacity to influence the policy of its allies and vice versa. It remains, astonishingly and perhaps absurdly, the only forum where the Europeans and the Americans can meet to discuss their politico-military problems and make provision for them; and if earlier hopes that these discussions might cover broader socioeconomic problems have so far borne little fruit, it is because so many other more appropriate institutions now exist to deal with them. Sheer inertia may keep the show on the road. But is that enough?

There is nothing wrong with inertia so long as it keeps the object moving in the right direction, and few would deny that continuing solidarity and cooperation between the United States and the nations of Europe remains an unexceptional goal. It might be argued that a military alliance is no longer the appropriate mechanism for persevering in that solidarity now that there is no longer a military threat, but it should be remembered that NATO was not just a military alliance in the first place. Today the threat that made its members emphasize their obligations under Article 5 at the expense of those under Article 2 no longer exists. So far as Article 2 is concerned, there is no reason why the membership of the alliance should not be indefinitely extended, and the more widely the better. Who could possibly object to "the further development of peaceful and friendly international relations by strengthening ... free institutions, by bringing about a better understanding of the principles upon which these institutions are founded and by promoting conditions of stability and well-being"? If that were all that was involved the partners could extend their family indefinitely and rub along forever. Even the obligations undertaken under Article 5, to regard an armed attack against one or more of the members as an attack against them all, are not especially rigorous: all that the parties undertake to do to assist the parties so attacked is to take "such action as [they] deem necessary, including the use of armed force, to restore and maintain international peace and security." What action is deemed necessary is left to the discretion of each party, and armed force is seen only as a possible option.

EVOLVE, NOT DISSOLVE

All might thus be well if the alliance could revert to the limited arrangements and expectations of its early months. But as was discovered in 1950, a credible guarantee that "includes the use of armed force" involves making joint military arrangements, designating and if necessary deploying forces well in advance; not just making paper promises. That was the unforgettable lesson of the 1930s, and presumably that is what aspiring candidates for membership in the alliance now expect. Any guarantee to defend an ally today involves making the military arrangements necessary to implement it. Robert E. Hunter, U.S. ambassador to NATO during the 1990s, expressed the hope that the difference between a "partner for peace" and membership in the alliance might become "razor-thin"; but it can be made so only by destroying the military credibility of the alliance itself. A huge gulf remains between, on the one hand, expressing ideological sympathy with another state and providing it with political support and economic help, and, on the other, committing one's armed forces, and risking the lives of one's civilians—and in the nuclear age the very survival of one's own society—for its physical defense.

Disagreements over the desirability of NATO extension have not so much divided the alliance as run through every NATO member state. The decision to extend was forced through by the United States, yet opposition to this step has been more extensive and vociferous in the United States than anywhere else. It has come not only from those who see it as an extension of the battle lines and the mind-set of the Cold War, but from those most concerned with the effectiveness and integrity of NATO as a functioning military entity. It has come also from those concerned for the political effectiveness of the alliance. It has been hard enough to create and maintain consensus among the original 15 members of the alliance on any issue beyond defense against the immediate threat to their territorial independence, if indeed on that. The advent of a group of members from central and eastern Europe, with a quite distinct geopolitical outlook, could make the task virtually impossible. And that should be borne in mind by those who now argue that NATO can justify itself only by assisting the United States in policing or pre-empting regional disputes—"out of area or out of business."

For of the four major subjects of discord among the allies—nuclear deterrence, detente, out-of-area commitment, and burden-sharing—only the last two remain. Burden-sharing is, and will continue to be, an unavoidable fact of life, but it has never been, and need not become, unmanageable. "Out of area," however, is now widely seen as the only justification for NATO's continuing existence by many in the United States who are still conscious, rightly or wrongly, of their responsibility for the preservation of some kind of world order. With the disappearance of the Soviet threat it is not clear what other purpose the alliance can still serve if not to share this burden.

But there are two major problems about this. The first is that only by a most imaginative interpretation of the text of the NATO treaty can alliance partners be held to have any "out of area" obligations at all. The second is that such operations demand a high degree of military cooperation and expertise such as can be expected only from a very few members of the alliance, whose intervention would probably be far more rapid and effective if it did not have to be sanctioned by a dozen or more reluctant allies and take place under the cumbrous umbrella of a NATO command structure.

Finally, there is the problem created by the evolution of the European Union itself. What territory will it cover, what powers will it have, and what attitude will it adopt towards the United States?

With the adoption of the Euro the European Union today seems to be developing a degree of economic cohesion that once seemed barely possible, and this will inevitably bring a certain degree of political unity in its train. Even the goal of a common foreign and defense policy, a European "Security and Defense Identity," now seems sufficiently attainable for NATO to be making provision for it within its own organization. Yet to many in Europe this goal still seems a distant one, and the more members that are admitted both to the union and to the alliance, the more distant it appears. It has been difficult enough during the past half-century to hammer out some kind of consensus about world events among London, Paris, Bonn, Rome, and Copenhagen, to say nothing of Ankara and Athens. Prague, Budapest, and Warsaw raise eyebrows. Add Vilnius and Bucharest, and the imagination begins to boggle. The most that can be expected is some kind of lowest common denominator that will always incline toward the kind of passivity with which the Europeans have infuriated their American allies ever since the 1950s. If the members of an enlarged European Union were ever to develop a single coherent defense and foreign policy, it would be as likely to find itself in opposition to that of the United States as in support of it.

None of this means that the alliance should be dissolved. It remains a uniquely appropriate framework within which the United States and the states of Europe can collaborate where collaboration is possible and coordinate their policies when collaboration is not in the cards. But it might be as well to define very much more closely what the alliance is now for. If it is to be just a community of like-minded states peacefully cooperating with and consulting each other as foreseen under Article 2, and in addition providing facilities for military cooperation by those members who wish to take part in out-of-area operations, well and good. It would continue to serve a valuable function for all its members, and be a stabilizing factor for the world as a whole. Then much of the huge and expensive infrastructure built up to implement the mutual military guarantees under Article 5 could be dismantled, and membership extended almost indefinitely to like-minded and contiguous nations.

But let us no longer pretend that this would be an effective military alliance as previously understood, whose members offer credible reciprocal guarantees to come to each other's defense. The alliance would still serve the goals set out in its original text, and even the wording of Article 5 would not be entirely invalid. The alliance can certainly continue as a successful marriage—but only if the partners know what they may now reasonably expect of one another.

Michael Howard is a former Regius Professor of Modern History at Oxford and Robert A. Lovett Professor of Military and Naval History at Yale. He is the life president of the International Institute of Strategic Studies.

The Unruled World

The Case for Good Enough Global Governance

Stewart Patrick

While campaigning for president in 2008, Barack Obama pledged to renovate the dilapidated multilateral edifice the United States had erected after World War II. He lionized the generation of Franklin Roosevelt, Harry Truman, and George Marshall for creating the United Nations, the Bretton Woods institutions, and NATO. Their genius, he said, was to recognize that "instead of constraining our power, these institutions magnified it." But the aging pillars of the postwar order were creaking and crumbling, Obama suggested, and so "to keep pace with the fast-moving threats we face," the world needed a new era of global institution building.

Five years into Obama's presidency, little progress has been made on that front, and few still expect it. Formal multilateral institutions continue to muddle along, holding their meetings and issuing their reports and taking some minor stabs at improving transnational problems at the margins. Yet despite the Obama administration's avowed ambition to integrate rising powers as full partners, there has been no movement to reform the composition of the UN Security Council to reflect new geopolitical realities. Meanwhile, the World Trade Organization (WTO) is comatose, NATO struggles to find its strategic purpose, and the International Energy Agency courts obsolescence by omitting China and India as members.

The demand for international cooperation has not diminished. In fact, it is greater than ever, thanks to deepening economic interdependence, worsening environmental degradation, proliferating transnational threats, and accelerating technological change. But effective multilateral responses are increasingly occurring outside formal institutions, as frustrated actors turn to more convenient, ad hoc venues. The relative importance of legal treaties and universal bodies such as the UN is declining, as the United States and other states rely more on regional organizations, "minilateral" cooperation among relevant states, codes of conduct, and partnerships with nongovernmental actors. And these trends are only going to continue. The future will see not the renovation or the construction of a glistening new international architecture but rather the continued spread of an unattractive but adaptable multilateral sprawl that delivers a partial measure of international cooperation through a welter of informal arrangements and piecemeal approaches.

"Global governance" is a slippery term. It refers not to world government (which nobody expects or wants anymore) but to something more practical: the collective effort by sovereign states, international organizations, and other nonstate actors to address common challenges and seize opportunities that transcend national frontiers. In domestic politics, governance is straightforward. It is provided by actual governments—formal, hierarchical institutions with the authority to establish and enforce binding rules. Governance in the international or transnational sphere, however, is more complex and ambiguous. There is some hierarchy—such as the special powers vested in the permanent members of the UN Security Council—but international politics remain anarchic, with the system composed of independent sovereign units that recognize no higher authority.

Cooperation under such anarchy is certainly possible. National governments often work together to establish common standards of behavior in spheres such as trade or security, embedding norms and rules in international institutions charged with providing global goods or mitigating global bads. But most cooperative multilateral bodies, even those binding under international law, lack real power to enforce compliance with collective decisions. What passes for governance is thus an ungainly patchwork of formal and informal institutions.

Alongside long-standing universal membership bodies, there are various regional institutions, multilateral alliances and security groups, standing consultative mechanisms, self-selecting clubs, ad hoc coalitions, issue-specific arrangements, transnational professional networks, technical standard-setting bodies, global action networks, and more. States are still the dominant actors, but nonstate actors increasingly help shape the global agenda, define new rules, and monitor compliance with international obligations.

The clutter is unsightly and unwieldy, but it has some advantages, as well. No single multilateral body could handle all the world's complex transnational problems, let alone do so effectively or nimbly. And the plurality of institutions and forums is not always dysfunctional, because it can offer states the chance to act relatively deftly and flexibly in responding to new challenges. But regardless of what one thinks of the current global disorder, it is clearly here to stay, and so the challenge is to make it work as well as possible.

BIG GAME

The centerpiece of contemporary global governance remains the UN, and the core of the UN system remains the Security Council—a standing committee including the most powerful countries in the world. In theory, the Security Council could serve as a venue for coordinating international responses to the world's most important threats to global order. In practice, however, it regularly disappoints—because the five permanent members (the United States, the United Kingdom, France, Russia, and China) often disagree and because their veto power allows the disagreements to block action. This has been true since the UN's inception, of course, but the Security Council's significance has diminished in recent decades as its composition has failed to track shifts in global power.

The Obama administration, like its predecessors, has flirted with the idea of pushing a charter amendment to update the Security Council's membership but has remained wary due to concerns that an enlarged Security Council, with new and more empowered members, might decrease U.S. influence and leverage. But even if Washington were to push hard for change, the status quo would be incredibly hard to overturn. Any expansion plan would require approval by two-thirds of the 193 members of the UN General Assembly, as well as domestic ratification by the five permanent members of the Security Council. And even those countries that favor expansion are deeply divided over which countries should benefit. So in practice, everyone pays lip service to enlargement while allowing the negotiations to drag on endlessly without any result.

This situation seems likely to persist, but at the cost of a deepening crisis of legitimacy, effectiveness, and compliance, as the Security Council's composition diverges ever further from the distribution of global power. Dissatisfied players could conceivably launch an all-out political assault on the institution, but they are much more likely to simply bypass the council, seeking alternative frameworks in which to address their concerns.

The dysfunction of the UN extends well beyond the Security Council, of course. Despite modest management reforms, the UN Secretariat and many UN agencies remain opaque, and their budgeting and operations are hamstrung by outdated personnel policies that encourage cronyism. Within the UN General Assembly, meanwhile, irresponsible actors who play to the galleries often dominate debates, and too many resolutions reflect encrusted regional and ideological blocs that somehow persist long after their sell-by date.

With the Security Council dominated by the old guard, rising powers have begun eyeing possible alternative venues for achieving influence and expressing their concerns. Shifts in global power have always ultimately produced shifts in the institutional superstructure, but what is distinctive today is the simultaneous emergence of multiple power centers with regional and potentially global aspirations. As the United States courts relative decline and Europe and Japan stagnate, China, India, Brazil, Russia, Turkey, Indonesia, and others are flexing their muscles, expanding their regional influence and insisting on greater voice within multilateral institutions.

Despite these geopolitical shifts, however, no coherent alternative to today's Western order has emerged. This is true even among the much-hyped BRICS: Brazil, Russia, India, China, and, since 2012, South Africa. These countries have always lacked a common vision, but at least initially, they shared a confidence born of economic dynamism and resentment over a global economy they perceived as stacked to favor the West. In recent years, the BRICS have staked out a few common positions. They all embrace traditional conceptions of state sovereignty and resist heavy-handed Western intervention. Their summit communiqués condemn the dollar's privileges as the world's main reserve currency and insist on accelerated governance reforms within the international financial institutions. The BRICS have also agreed to create a full-fledged BRICS bank to provide development aid to countries and for issues the bloc defines as priorities, without the conditionality imposed by Western donors.

Some observers anticipate the BRICS' emerging as an independent caucus and center of gravity within the G-20, rivaling the G-7 nations. But any such bifurcation of the world order between developed and major developing powers seems a distant prospect, for as much divides the BRICS as binds them. China and Russia have no interest in seeing any of their putative partners join them as permanent Security Council members; China and India are emerging strategic competitors with frontier disputes and divergent maritime interests; and China and Russia have their own tensions along the Siberian border. Differences in their internal regimes may also constrain their collaboration. India, Brazil, and South Africa—boisterous multiparty democracies all—have formed a coalition of their own (the India–Brazil–South Africa Dialogue Forum, or IBSA), as have China and Russia (the Shanghai Cooperation Organization).

Conflicting economic interests also complicate intra-BRICS relations, something that might increase as the countries' growth slows.

WELCOME TO THE G-X WORLD

The analysts Ian Bremmer and David Gordon have written about the emergence of a "G-Zero world," in which collective global leadership is almost impossible thanks to a global diffusion of power among countries with widely divergent interests. But what really marks the contemporary era is not the absence of multilateralism but its astonishing diversity. Collective action is no longer focused solely, or even primarily, on the UN and other universal, treaty-based institutions, nor even on a single apex forum such as the G-20. Rather, governments have taken to operating in many venues simultaneously, participating in a bewildering array of issue-specific networks and partnerships whose membership varies based on situational interests, shared values, and relevant capabilities.

A hallmark of this "G-X" world is the temporary coalition of strange bedfellows. Consider the multinational antipiracy armada that has emerged in the Indian Ocean. This loosely coordinated flotilla involves naval vessels from not only the United States and its NATO allies but also China, India, Indonesia, Iran, Japan, Malaysia, Russia, Saudi Arabia, South Korea, and Yemen. These countries might disagree on many issues, but they have found common cause in securing sealanes off the African coast.

At the same time, the G-X world permits the United States to strengthen its links within the traditional West. Take the surprisingly resilient G-8, composed of the United States, Japan, Germany, France, the United Kingdom, Italy, Canada, and Russia (plus the EU). For years, pundits have predicted the G-8's demise, and yet it still moves. The G-8 allows advanced market democracies to coordinate their positions on sensitive political and security issues—just as the parallel financially focused G-7 permits them to harmonize their macroeconomic policies. With the exception of authoritarian Russia, unwisely added in 1997, G-8 members share similar worldviews and values, strategic interests, and major policy preferences. This like-mindedness facilitates policy coordination on matters ranging from human rights to humanitarian intervention, rogue states to regional stability.

The wealthy G-8 members also possess distinctive assets—financial, diplomatic, military, and ideological—to deploy in the service of their convictions. At the Deauville summit of May 2011, the G-8 moved quickly to offer diplomatic support and material assistance to the Arab Spring countries. That action reaffirmed the G-8 as a practical and symbolic anchor of the Western liberal order while reminding the world that the G-8 remains the overwhelming source of official development assistance. In global governance, as elsewhere, necessity is the mother of invention, and the global credit crisis that struck with full force in 2008 led to the rise to prominence of a relatively new international grouping, the G-20. Facing the potential meltdown of the international financial system, leaders of the world's major economies—both developed and developing—shared an overriding interest in avoiding a second Great Depression. Stuck in the same lifeboat, they assented to a slew of institutional innovations, including elevating the G-20 finance ministers' group to the leaders' level, creating an exclusive global crisis-response committee.

The G-20 quickly racked up some notable achievements. It injected unprecedented liquidity into the world economy through coordinated national actions, including some $5 trillion in stimulus at the London summit of April 2009. It created the Financial Stability Board, charged with developing new regulatory standards for systemically important financial institutions, and insisted on new bank capital account requirements under the Basel III agreement. It revitalized and augmented the coffers of the once-moribund International Monetary Fund and negotiated governance reforms within the World Bank and the IMF to give greater voice to emerging economies. And its members adopted "standstill" provisions to avoid a recurrence of the ruinous tit-for-tat trade protectionism of the 1930s.

As the immediate panic receded and an uneven global recovery took hold, however, narrow national interests again came to the fore, slowing the G-20's momentum. For the past four years, the G-20—whose heterogeneous members possess diverse values, political systems, and levels of development—has struggled to evolve from a short-term crisis manager to a longer-term steering group for the global economy. The reform of major international financial institutions has also stalled, as established (notably European) powers resist reallocating voting weight and governing board seats. So what looked for a brief moment like the dawn of a newly preeminent global forum proved to be just one more outlet store in the sprawl.

GOVERNANCE IN PIECES

For much of the past two decades, UN mega-conferences dominated multilateral diplomacy. But when it comes to multilateralism, bigger is rarely better, and the era of the mega-conference is ending as major powers recognize the futility of negotiating comprehensive international agreements among 193 UN member states, in the full glare of the media and alongside tens of thousands of activists, interest groups, and hangers-on. Countries will continue to assemble for annual confabs, such as the Conference of the Parties to the UN Framework Convention on Climate Change (UNFCCC), in the Sisyphean quest to secure "binding" commitments from developed and developing countries. But that circus will increasingly become a sideshow, as the action shifts to less formal settings and narrower groupings of the relevant and capable. Already, the 17 largest greenhouse gas emitters have created the Major Economies Forum on Energy and Climate, seeking breakthroughs outside the lumbering UNFCCC. To date, the forum has underdelivered. But more tangible progress has occurred through parallel national efforts, as states pledge to undertake a menu of domestic actions, which they subsequently submit to the forum for collective review.

There is a more general lesson here. Faced with fiendishly complex issues, such as climate change, transnational networks of government officials now seek incremental progress by disaggregating those issues into manageable chunks and agreeing to coordinate action on specific agenda items. Call it "global governance in pieces." For climate change, this means abandoning the quest for an elusive soup-to-nuts agreement to mitigate and adapt to global warming. Instead, negotiators pursue separate initiatives, such as phasing out wasteful fossil fuel subsidies, launching minilateral clean technology partnerships, and expanding the UN Collaborative Program on Reducing Emissions from Deforestation and Forest Degradation in Developing Countries, among other worthwhile schemes. The result is not a unitary international regime grounded in a single institution or treaty but a cluster of complementary activities that political scientists call a "regime complex."

Something similar is happening in global health, where the once-premier World Health Organization now shares policy space and a division of labor with other major organizations, such as the World Bank; specialized UN agencies, such as UNAIDS; public-private partnerships, such as the GAVI Alliance (formerly called the Global Alliance for Vaccines and Immunization); philanthropic organizations, such as the Bill and Melinda Gates Foundation; consultative bodies, such as the eight-nation (plus the EU) Global Health Security Initiative; and multi-stakeholder bodies, such as the Global Fund to Fight AIDS, Tuberculosis and Malaria. The upshot is a disaggregated system of global health governance.

Sometimes, the piecemeal approach may be able to achieve more than its stagnant universalist alternative. Given the failure of the WTO's Doha Round, for example, the United States and other nations have turned to preferential trade agreements in order to spur further liberalization of commerce. Some are bilateral, such as the U.S.–South Korean pact. But others involve multiple countries. These include two initiatives that constitute the centerpiece of Obama's second-term trade agenda: the Trans-Pacific Partnership and the Transatlantic Trade and Investment Partnership. The administration describes each as a steppingstone toward global liberalization. And yet future WTO negotiations will likely take a disaggregated form, as subsets of WTO members move forward on more manageable specific issues (such as public procurement or investment) while avoiding those lightning-rod topics (such as trade in agriculture) that have repeatedly stymied comprehensive trade negotiations.

THE RISE OF THE REGIONS

Ad hoc coalitions and minilateral networks are not the only global governance innovations worthy of mention. Regional organizations are also giving universal membership bodies a run for their money, raising the question of how to make sure they harmonize and complement the UN system rather than undermine it.

This dilemma is older than often assumed. In the months leading up to the San Francisco conference of 1945, at which the UN was established, U.S. and British postwar planners debated whether regional bodies ought to be given formal, even independent, standing within the UN (something British Prime Minister Winston Churchill, among others, had proposed). Most U.S. negotiators were adamantly opposed, fearing that an overtly regional thrust would detract from the UN's coherence or even fracture it into rival blocs. In the end, the Americans' universal vision prevailed. Still, Chapter 8 of the UN Charter acknowledges a legitimate subordinate role for regional organizations.

What few in San Francisco could have envisioned was the dramatic proliferation and increasingly sophisticated capabilities of regional and subregional arrangements, which today number in the hundreds. These bodies play an ever more important role in managing cross-border challenges, facilitating trade, and promoting regional security, often in partnership with the UN and other universal organizations. Consider peacekeeping on the African continent. Alongside classic UN operations, we now see a variety of hybrid models, in which the UN Security Council authorizes an observer or peacekeeping mission, which is then implemented by an ad hoc coalition (as in the NATO-led mission in Libya), a regional organization (as in the African Union Mission in Somalia, or AMISOM), or some combination of the two.

This budding role for regional organizations poses policy conundrums. One is whether regional organizations ought to be allowed to serve as gatekeepers for UN-mandated enforcement actions. This contentious issue arose in 2011 after NATO launched Operation Unified Protector in Libya, with the authorization of the UN Security Council and the diplomatic support of the Arab League but not, critically, of the African Union. In January 2012, South African President Jacob Zuma, with South Africa occupying the rotating presidency of the UN Security Council, blasted the Western powers for exceeding the intent of Resolution 1973 in treating their mandate to protect Libyan civilians as a license for regime change. "Africa," he insisted, "must not be a playground for furthering the interests of other regions ever again." Seeking to tighten the relationship between the UN Security Council and regional organizations, Zuma introduced a resolution proposing a system of codetermination for authorizing enforcement actions. Predictably, this gambit met with solid opposition from the five permanent members, and some dismissed the move as populist showboating. But Zuma had given voice to a larger concern: the perceived legitimacy and practical success of international interventions increasingly depends on support from relevant regional organizations.

Given how overstretched the UN and other global bodies can become, rising regionalism has distinct benefits. Regional bodies are often more familiar with the underlying sources of local conflicts, and they may be more sensitive to and invested in potential solutions. But they are in no position to replace the UN entirely. To begin with, regional organizations vary widely in their aspirations, mandates, capabilities, and activities. They are also vulnerable to the same collective-action problems that bedevil the UN. Their members are often tempted to adopt bland, lowest-common-denominator positions or to try to free-ride on the contributions of others. Local hegemons may seek to hijack them for narrow purposes. The ambitions of regional organizations can also outstrip their ability to deliver. Although the African Union has created the Peace and Security Council, for instance, the organization's capacity to conduct peacekeeping operations remains hamstrung by institutional, professional, technical, material, and logistical shortcomings. Accordingly, burden sharing between the UN and regional organizations can easily devolve into burden shifting, as the world invests unprepared regional bodies with unrealistic expectations.

GOVERNING THE CONTESTED COMMONS

If one major problem in contemporary global governance is the floundering of existing institutions when dealing with traditional challenges, another and equally worrisome problem is the lack of any serious institutional mechanism for dealing with untraditional challenges. The gap between the demand for and the supply of global governance is greatest when it comes to the global commons, those spaces no nation controls but on which all rely for security and prosperity. The most important of these are the maritime, outer space, and cyberspace domains, which carry the flows of goods, data, capital, people, and ideas on which globalization rests. Ensuring free and unencumbered access to these realms is therefore a core interest not only of the United States but of most other nations as well.

For almost seven decades, the United States has provided security for the global commons and, in so doing, has bolstered world order. Supremacy at sea—and, more recently, in outer space and online—has also conferred strategic advantages on the United States, allowing it to project power globally. But as the commons become crowded and cutthroat, that supremacy is fading. Rising powers, as well as nonstate actors from corporations to criminals, are challenging long-standing behavioral norms and deploying asymmetric capabilities to undercut U.S. advantages. Preserving the openness, stability, and resilience of the global commons will require the United States to forge agreement among like-minded nations, rising powers, and private stakeholders on new rules of the road.

From China to Iran, for example, rising powers are seeking blue-water capabilities or employing asymmetric strategies to deny the United States and other countries access to their regional waters, jeopardizing the freedom of the seas. The greatest flashpoint today is in the South China Sea, through which more than $5 trillion worth of commerce passes each year. There, China is locked in dangerous sovereignty disputes with Brunei, Malaysia, the Philippines, Taiwan, and Vietnam over some 1.3 million square miles of ocean, the contested islands therein, and the exploitation of undersea oil and gas reserves. Beijing's assertiveness poses grave risks for regional stability.

Most dangerous would be a direct U.S.Chinese naval clash, perhaps in response to U.S. freedom-of-navigation exercises in China's littoral waters or the reckless actions of a U.S. treaty ally or strategic partner.

Geopolitical and economic competition has also heated up in the warming Arctic, as nations wrangle over rights to extended continental shelves, new sea routes over Asia and North America, and the exploitation of fossil fuel and mineral deposits. To date, cooler heads have prevailed. In 2008, the five Arctic nations—Canada, Denmark, Norway, Russia, and the United States—signed the Ilulissat Declaration, affirming their commitment to address any overlapping claims in a peaceful and orderly manner. Some experts contend that the Arctic needs a comprehensive multilateral treaty to reconcile competing sovereignty claims, handle navigational issues, facilitate collective energy development, manage fisheries, and address environmental concerns. A more productive strategy would be to bolster the role of the Arctic Council, composed of the five Arctic nations plus Finland, Iceland, Sweden, and several indigenous peoples' organizations. Although this forum has historically avoided contentious boundary and legal disputes, it could help codify guidelines on oil and gas development, sponsor collaborative mapping of the continental shelf, create a regional monitoring network, and modernize systems for navigation, traffic management, and environmental protection.

The single most important step the United States could take to strengthen ocean governance, including in the Arctic, would be to finally accede to the UN Convention on the Law of the Sea, as recommended by the last four U.S. presidents, U.S. military leaders, industry, and environmental groups. Beyond defining states' rights and responsibilities in territorial seas and exclusive economic zones and clarifying the rules for transit through international straits, UNCLOS provides a forum for dispute resolution on ocean-related issues, including claims to extended continental shelves. As a nonmember, the United States forfeits its chance to participate in the last great partitioning of sovereign space on earth, which would grant it jurisdiction over vast areas along its Arctic, Atlantic, Gulf, and Pacific coasts. Nor can it serve on the International Seabed Authority, where it would enjoy a permanent seat with an effective veto. By remaining apart, the United States not only undercuts its national interests but also undermines its perceived commitment to a rule-based international order and emboldens revisionist regional powers. Both China in East Asia and Russia in the Arctic have taken advantage of the United States' absence to advance outrageous sovereignty claims.

At the same time, U.S. accession to the treaty would be no panacea. This is particularly true in East Asia, where China has been unwilling to submit its claims to binding arbitration under UNCLOS. Ultimately, the peaceful resolution of competing regional claims will require China and its neighbors in the Association of Southeast Asian Nations to agree on a binding code of conduct addressing matters of territorial jurisdiction and joint exploitation of undersea resources. This is something that Beijing has strenuously resisted, but it seems inevitable if the Chinese government wants to preserve the credibility of its "peaceful rise" rhetoric.

THE FINAL FRONTIER

The international rules governing the uses of outer space have also become outdated, as that domain becomes, in the words of former U.S. Deputy Secretary of Defense William Lynn, more "congested, contested, and competitive." As nations and private corporations vie for scarce orbital slots for their satellites and for slices of a finite radio-frequency spectrum, the number of actors operating in space has skyrocketed. Already, nine countries and the European Space Agency have orbital launch capabilities, and nearly 60 nations or government consortiums regulate civil, commercial, and military satellites. The proliferation of vehicles and space debris—including more than 22,000 orbiting objects larger than a softball—has increased the risk of catastrophic collisions. More worrisome, geopolitical competition among spacefaring nations, both established and emerging, raises the specter of an arms race in space.

Yet so far at least, there is little global consensus on what kind of regulatory regime would best ensure the stability and sustainable use of earth's final frontier. The basic convention governing national conduct in outer space remains the Outer Space Treaty of 1967. Although it establishes useful principles (such as a prohibition on sovereignty claims in space), that treaty lacks a dispute-resolution mechanism, is silent on space debris and how to avoid collisions, and inadequately addresses interference with the space assets of other countries.

To address these shortcomings, various parties have suggested options ranging from a binding multilateral treaty banning space weapons to an informal agreement on standards of behavior. Given the problems with a treaty-based approach, the Obama administration has wisely focused on seeking a nonbinding international code of conduct for outer space activities that would establish broad principles and parameters for responsible behavior in space. Such a voluntary code would carry a lesser obligation than a legally binding multilateral treaty, but it offers the best chance to establish new behavioral norms in the short term. Washington should also consider sponsoring a standing minilateral consultative forum of spacefaring nations.

LOST IN CYBERSPACE

Cyberspace differs from the oceans or outer space in that its physical infrastructure is located primarily in sovereign states and in private hands—creating obvious risks of interference by parties pursuing their own interests. Since the dawn of the digital age, the United States has been the premier champion of an open, decentralized, and secure cyberspace that remains largely private. This posture is consistent with the long-standing U.S. belief that the free flow of information and ideas is a core component of a free, just, and open world and an essential bulwark against authoritarianism. But this vision of global governance in cyberspace is now under threat from three directions.

The first is the demand by many developing and authoritarian countries that regulation of the Internet be transferred from ICANN, the Internet Corporation for Assigned Names and Numbers—an independent, nonprofit corporation based in Los Angeles, loosely supervised by the U.S. Department of Commerce—to the UN's ITU (International Telecommunication Union). The second is a growing epidemic of cybercrime, consisting mostly of attempts to steal proprietary information from private-sector actors. Thanks to sophisticated computer viruses, worms, and botnets, what might be termed "cyber public health" has deteriorated dramatically. And there is no cyberspace equivalent to the World Health Organization for dealing with such dangers.

The third major flashpoint is the growing specter of cyberwar among sovereign states. Dozens of nations have begun to develop doctrines and capabilities for conducting so-called information operations, not only to infiltrate but if necessary to disrupt and destroy the critical digital infrastructure (both military and civilian) of their adversaries. Yet there is no broadly accepted definition of a cyberattack, much less consensus on the range of permissible responses; the normative and legal framework governing cyberwar has lagged behind cyberweapons' development and use. Traditional forms of deterrence and retaliation are also complicated, given the difficulty of attributing attacks to particular perpetrators.

No single UN treaty could simultaneously regulate cyberwarfare, counter cybercrime, and protect the civil liberties of Internet users. Liberal and authoritarian regimes disagree on the definition of "cybersecurity" and how to achieve it, with the latter generally seeing the free exchange of ideas and information not as a core value but as a potential threat to their stability, and there are various practical hurdles to including cyberweapons in traditional arms control and nonproliferation negotiations. So a piecemeal approach to governance in cyberspace seems more realistic. States will need to negotiate norms of responsibility for cyberattacks and criteria for retaliation. They should also develop transparency and confidence-building measures and agree to preserve humanitarian fundamentals in the event of a cyberwar, avoiding attacks on "root" servers, which constitute the backbone of the Internet, and prohibiting all denial-of-service attacks, which can cripple the Internet infrastructure of the targeted countries. Washington might start advancing such an agenda through a coalition of like-minded states—akin to the Financial Action Task Force or the Proliferation Security Initiative—expanding membership outward as feasible.

TECHNOLOGY AND THE FRONTIERS OF GLOBAL GOVERNANCE

The history of global governance is the story of adaptation to new technologies. As breakthroughs have been made, sovereign governments have sought common standards and rules to facilitate cooperation and mitigate conflict. For example, we now take for granted the world's division into 24 separate time zones, with Greenwich

Mean Time as the base line, but in the middle of the nineteenth century, the United States alone had 144 local time zones. It was only the need to standardize train and shipping schedules in the late nineteenth century that convinced major countries to synchronize their time.

Today, the furious pace of technological change risks leaving global governance in the dust. The growing gap between what technological advances permit and what the international system is prepared to regulate can be seen in multiple areas, from drones and synthetic biology to nanotechnology and geoengineering.

When it comes to drones, the United States has struggled mightily to develop its own legal rationale for targeted assassinations. Initial foreign objections to U.S. drone strikes were concentrated within the target countries, but increasingly, their use has been challenged both domestically and internationally, and the rapid spread of drone technology to both state and nonstate actors makes it imperative to create clear rules for their use—and soon.

Rapid advances in biotechnology could pose even greater long-term threats. Scientists today are in a position to create new biological systems by manipulating genetic material. Such "synthetic biology" has tremendous therapeutic and public health potential but could also cause great harm, with rogue states or rogue scientists fabricating deadly pathogens or other bioweapons. At present, only an incomplete patchwork of regulations exist to prevent such risks. Nor are there any international regulatory arrangements to govern research on and uses of nanotechnology: the process of manipulating materials at the atomic or molecular level. Where regulation exists, it is performed primarily on a national basis; in the United States, for example, this function is carried out jointly by the Environmental Protection Agency, the Food and Drug Administration, and the National Institute of Standards and Technology. To make things even more complicated, most research and investment in this area is currently carried out by the private sector, which has little incentive to consider potential threats to public safety.

Finally, the threat of uncoordinated efforts at geoengineering—the attempt to slow or reverse global warming through large-scale tinkering with the planet's climate system—also demands regulation. Such schemes include seeding the world's oceans with iron filings (as one freelancing U.S. scientist attempted in 2012), deflecting solar radiation through a system of space-based mirrors, and preventing the release of methane held in tundras and the ocean. Long dismissed as fanciful, such attempts to reengineer the earth's atmosphere are suddenly being taken seriously by at least some mainstream experts. As warming proceeds, countries and private actors will be increasingly tempted to take matters into their own hands. Only proper regulation has a chance of ensuring that these uncoordinated efforts do not go badly awry, with potentially disastrous consequences.

"GOOD ENOUGH" GLOBAL GOVERNANCE

As all these examples highlight, demand for effective global governance continues to outstrip supply, and the gap is growing. Absent dramatic crises, multilateral institutions have been painfully slow and lumbering in their response. So even as they try to revitalize the existing international order, diplomats and other interested parties need to turn to other, complementary frameworks for collective action, including ad hoc coalitions of the willing, regional and subregional institutions, public-private arrangements, and informal codes of conduct. The resulting jerry-rigged structure for global cooperation will not be aesthetically pleasing, but it might at least get some useful things done.

A decade ago, the Harvard scholar Merilee Grindle launched a broadside against the lengthy list of domestic good-governance reforms that the World Bank and other agencies insisted were necessary to encourage growth and reduce poverty in developing countries. She implored international donors to put their long, well-intentioned checklists aside and focus instead on "good enough governance." Rather than try to tackle all problems at once, she suggested, aid agencies should focus on achieving the minimal institutional requirements for progress. This advice to lower expectations and start with the necessary and possible is even more applicable in the international sphere, given all the obstacles in the way of sweeping institutional reform there. For the Obama administration and its colleagues and successors, achieving some measure of "good enough" global governance might be less satisfying than trying to replay the glory days of the Truman administration. But it would be much better than nothing, and it might even work.

STEWART PATRICK is a **Senior Fellow and Director of the International Institutions and Global Governance Program** at the Council on Foreign Relations.

© Foreign Affairs

The Return of Geopolitics

The Revenge of the Revisionist Powers

Walter Russell Mead

Russian servicemen in historical uniforms take part in a military parade in Moscow's Red Square, November 3, 2011.

So far, the year 2014 has been a tumultuous one, as geopolitical rivalries have stormed back to center stage. Whether it is Russian forces seizing Crimea, China making aggressive claims in its coastal waters, Japan responding with an increasingly assertive strategy of its own, or Iran trying to use its alliances with Syria and Hezbollah to dominate the Middle East, old-fashioned power plays are back in international relations.

The United States and the EU, at least, find such trends disturbing. Both would rather move past geopolitical questions of territory and military power and focus instead on ones of world order and global governance: trade liberalization, nuclear nonproliferation, human rights, the rule of law, climate change, and so on. Indeed, since the end of the Cold War, the most important objective of U.S. and EU foreign policy has been to shift international relations away from zero-sum issues toward win-win ones. To be dragged back into old-school contests such as that in Ukraine doesn't just divert time and energy away from those important questions; it also changes the character of international politics. As the atmosphere turns dark, the task of promoting and maintaining world order grows more daunting.

But Westerners should never have expected old-fashioned geopolitics to go away. They did so only because they fundamentally misread what the collapse of the Soviet Union meant: the ideological triumph of liberal capitalist democracy over communism, not the obsolescence of hard power. China, Iran, and Russia never bought into the geopolitical settlement that followed the Cold War, and they are making increasingly forceful attempts to overturn it. That process will not be peaceful, and whether or not the revisionists succeed, their efforts have already shaken the balance of power and changed the dynamics of international politics.

A FALSE SENSE OF SECURITY

When the Cold War ended, many Americans and Europeans seemed to think that the most vexing geopolitical questions had largely been settled. With the exception of a handful of relatively minor problems, such as the woes of the former Yugoslavia and the Israeli-Palestinian dispute, the biggest issues in world politics, they assumed, would no longer concern boundaries, military bases, national self-determination, or spheres of influence.

One can't blame people for hoping. The West's approach to the realities of the post–Cold War world has made a great deal of sense, and it is hard to see how world peace can ever be achieved without replacing geopolitical competition with the construction of a liberal world order. Still, Westerners often forget that this project rests on the particular geopolitical foundations laid in the early 1990s.

In Europe, the post–Cold War settlement involved the unification of Germany, the dismemberment of the Soviet Union, and the integration of the former Warsaw Pact states and the Baltic republics into NATO and the EU. In the Middle East, it entailed the dominance of Sunni powers that were allied with the United States (Saudi Arabia, its Gulf allies, Egypt, and Turkey) and the double containment of Iran and Iraq. In Asia, it meant the uncontested dominance of the United States, embedded in a series of security relationships with Japan, South Korea, Australia, Indonesia, and other allies.

This settlement reflected the power realities of the day, and it was only as stable as the relationships that held it up. Unfortunately, many observers conflated the temporary geopolitical conditions of the post–Cold War world with the presumably more final outcome of the ideological struggle between liberal democracy and Soviet communism. The political scientist Francis Fukuyama's famous formulation that the end of the Cold War meant "the end of history" was a statement about ideology. But for many people, the collapse of the Soviet Union didn't just mean that humanity's ideological struggle was over for good; they thought geopolitics itself had also come to a permanent end.

At first glance, this conclusion looks like an extrapolation of Fukuyama's argument rather than a distortion of it. After all, the idea of the end of history has rested on the geopolitical consequences of ideological struggles ever since the German philosopher Georg Wilhelm Friedrich Hegel first expressed it at the beginning of the nineteenth century. For Hegel, it was the Battle of Jena, in 1806, that rang the curtain down on the war of ideas. In Hegel's eyes, Napoleon Bonaparte's utter destruction of the Prussian army in that brief campaign represented the triumph of the French Revolution over the best army that prerevolutionary Europe could produce. This spelled an end to history, Hegel argued, because in the future, only states that adopted the principles and techniques of revolutionary France would be able to compete and survive.

Adapted to the post–Cold War world, this argument was taken to mean that in the future, states would have to adopt the principles of liberal capitalism to keep up. Closed, communist societies, such as the Soviet Union, had shown themselves to be too uncreative and unproductive to compete economically and militarily with liberal states. Their political regimes were also shaky, since no social form other than liberal democracy provided enough freedom and dignity for a contemporary society to remain stable.

To fight the West successfully, you would have to become like the West, and if that happened, you would become the kind of wishy-washy, pacifistic milquetoast society that didn't want to fight about anything at all. The only remaining dangers to world peace would come from rogue states such as North Korea, and although such countries might have the will to challenge the West, they would be too crippled by their obsolete political and social structures to rise above the nuisance level (unless they developed nuclear weapons, of course). And thus former communist states, such as Russia, faced a choice. They could jump on the modernization bandwagon and become liberal, open, and pacifistic, or they could cling bitterly to their guns and their culture as the world passed them by.

At first, it all seemed to work. With history over, the focus shifted from geopolitics to development economics and nonproliferation, and the bulk of foreign policy came to center on questions such as climate change and trade. The conflation of the end of geopolitics and the end of history offered an especially enticing prospect to the United States: the idea that the country could start putting less into the international system and taking out more. It could shrink its defense spending, cut the State Department's appropriations, lower its profile in foreign hotspots—and the world would just go on becoming more prosperous and more free.

This vision appealed to both liberals and conservatives in the United States. The administration of President Bill Clinton, for example, cut both the Defense Department's and the State Department's budgets and was barely able to persuade Congress to keep paying U.S. dues to the UN. At the same time, policymakers assumed that the international system would become stronger and wider-reaching while continuing to be conducive to U.S. interests. Republican neo-isolationists, such as former Representative Ron Paul of Texas, argued that given the absence of serious geopolitical challenges, the United States could dramatically cut both military spending and foreign aid while continuing to benefit from the global economic system.

After 9/11, President George W. Bush based his foreign policy on the belief that Middle Eastern terrorists constituted a uniquely dangerous opponent, and he launched what he said would be a long war against them. In some respects, it appeared that the world was back in the realm of history. But the Bush administration's belief that democracy could be implanted quickly in the Arab Middle East, starting with Iraq, testified to a deep conviction that the overall tide of events was running in America's favor.

President Barack Obama built his foreign policy on the conviction that the "war on terror" was overblown, that history really was over, and that, as in the Clinton years, the United States' most important priorities involved promoting the liberal world order, not playing classical geopolitics. The administration articulated an extremely ambitious agenda in support of that order: blocking Iran's drive for nuclear weapons, solving the Israeli-Palestinian conflict, negotiating a global climate change treaty, striking Pacific and Atlantic trade deals, signing arms control treaties with Russia, repairing U.S. relations with the Muslim world, promoting gay rights, restoring trust with European allies, and ending the war in Afghanistan. At the same time, however, Obama planned to cut defense spending dramatically and reduced U.S. engagement in key world theaters, such as Europe and the Middle East.

AN AXIS OF WEEVILS?

All these happy convictions are about to be tested. Twenty-five years after the fall of the Berlin Wall, whether one focuses on the rivalry between the EU and Russia over Ukraine, which led Moscow to seize Crimea; the intensifying competition between China and Japan in East Asia; or the subsuming of sectarian conflict into international rivalries and civil wars in the Middle East, the world is looking less post-historical by the day. In very different ways, with very different objectives, China, Iran, and Russia are all pushing back against the political settlement of the Cold War.

The relationships among those three revisionist powers are complex. In the long run, Russia fears the rise of China. Tehran's worldview has little in common with that of either Beijing or Moscow. Iran and Russia are oil-exporting countries and like the price of oil to be high; China is a net consumer and wants prices low. Political instability in the Middle East can work to Iran's and Russia's advantage but poses large risks for China. One should not speak of a strategic alliance among them, and over time, particularly if they succeed in undermining U.S. influence in Eurasia, the tensions among them are more likely to grow than shrink.

What binds these powers together, however, is their agreement that the status quo must be revised. Russia wants to reassemble as much of the Soviet Union as it can. China has no intention of contenting itself with a secondary role in global affairs, nor will it accept the current degree of U.S. influence in Asia and the territorial status quo there. Iran wishes to replace the current order in the Middle East—led by Saudi Arabia and dominated by Sunni Arab states—with one centered on Tehran.

Leaders in all three countries also agree that U.S. power is the chief obstacle to achieving their revisionist goals. Their hostility toward Washington and its order is both offensive and defensive: not only do they hope that the decline of U.S. power will make it easier to reorder their regions, but they also worry that Washington might try to overthrow them should discord within their countries grow. Yet the revisionists want to avoid direct confrontations with the United States, except in rare circumstances when the odds are strongly in their favor (as in Russia's 2008 invasion of Georgia and its occupation and annexation of Crimea this year). Rather than challenge the status quo head on, they seek to chip away at the norms and relationships that sustain it.

Since Obama has been president, each of these powers has pursued a distinct strategy in light of its own strengths and weaknesses. China, which has the greatest capabilities of the three, has paradoxically been the most frustrated. Its efforts to assert itself in its region have only tightened the links between the United States and its Asian allies and intensified nationalism in Japan. As Beijing's capabilities grow, so will its sense of frustration. China's surge in power will be matched by a surge in Japan's resolve, and tensions in Asia will be more likely to spill over into global economics and politics.

Iran, by many measures the weakest of the three states, has had the most successful record. The combination of the United States' invasion of Iraq and then its premature withdrawal has enabled Tehran to cement deep and enduring ties with significant power centers across the Iraqi border, a development that has changed both the sectarian and the political balance of power in the region. In Syria, Iran, with the help of its longtime ally Hezbollah, has been able to reverse the military tide and prop up the government of Bashar al-Assad in the face of strong opposition from the U.S. government. This triumph of realpolitik has added considerably to Iran's power and prestige. Across the region, the Arab Spring has weakened Sunni regimes, further tilting the balance in Iran's favor. So has the growing split among Sunni governments over what to do about the Muslim Brotherhood and its offshoots and adherents.

Russia, meanwhile, has emerged as the middling revisionist: more powerful than Iran but weaker than China, more successful than China at geopolitics but less successful than Iran. Russia has been moderately effective at driving wedges between Germany and the United States, but Russian President Vladimir Putin's preoccupation with rebuilding the Soviet Union has been hobbled by the sharp limits of his country's economic power. To build a real Eurasian bloc, as Putin dreams of doing, Russia would have to underwrite the bills of the former Soviet republics—something it cannot afford to do.

Nevertheless, Putin, despite his weak hand, has been remarkably successful at frustrating Western projects on former Soviet territory. He has stopped NATO expansion dead in its tracks. He has dismembered Georgia, brought Armenia into his orbit, tightened his hold on Crimea, and, with his Ukrainian adventure, dealt the West an unpleasant and humiliating surprise. From the Western point of view, Putin appears to be condemning his country to an ever-darker future of poverty and marginalization. But Putin doesn't believe that history has ended, and from his perspective, he has solidified his power at home and reminded hostile foreign powers that the Russian bear still has sharp claws.

THE POWERS THAT BE

The revisionist powers have such varied agendas and capabilities that none can provide the kind of systematic and global opposition that the Soviet Union did. As a result, Americans have been slow to realize that these states have undermined the Eurasian geopolitical order in ways that complicate U.S. and European efforts to construct a post-historical, win-win world.

Still, one can see the effects of this revisionist activity in many places. In East Asia, China's increasingly assertive stance has yet to yield much concrete geopolitical progress, but it has fundamentally altered the political dynamic in the region with the fastest-growing economies on earth. Asian politics today revolve around national rivalries, conflicting territorial claims, naval buildups, and similar historical issues. The nationalist revival in Japan, a direct response to China's agenda, has set up a process in which rising nationalism in one country feeds off the same in the other. China and Japan are escalating their rhetoric, increasing their military budgets, starting bilateral crises with greater frequency, and fixating more and more on zero-sum competition.

Although the EU remains in a post-historical moment, the non-EU republics of the former Soviet Union are living in a very different age. In the last few years, hopes of transforming the former Soviet Union into a post-historical region have faded. The Russian occupation of Ukraine is only the latest in a series of steps that have turned eastern Europe into a zone of sharp geopolitical conflict and made stable and effective democratic governance impossible outside the Baltic states and Poland.

In the Middle East, the situation is even more acute. Dreams that the Arab world was approaching a democratic tipping point—dreams that informed U.S. policy under both the Bush and the Obama administrations—have faded. Rather than building a liberal order in the region, U.S. policymakers are grappling with the unraveling of the state system that dates back to the 1916 Sykes-Picot agreement, which divided up the Middle Eastern provinces of the Ottoman Empire, as governance erodes in Iraq, Lebanon, and Syria. Obama has done his best to separate the geopolitical issue of Iran's surging power across the region from the question of its compliance with the Nuclear Nonproliferation Treaty, but Israeli and Saudi fears about Iran's regional ambitions are making that harder to do. Another obstacle to striking agreements with Iran is Russia, which has used its seat on the UN Security Council and support for Assad to set back U.S. goals in Syria.

Russia sees its influence in the Middle East as an important asset in its competition with the United States. This does not mean that Moscow will reflexively oppose U.S. goals on every occasion, but it does mean that the win-win outcomes that Americans so eagerly seek will sometimes be held hostage to Russian geopolitical interests. In deciding how hard to press Russia over Ukraine, for example, the White House cannot avoid calculating the impact on Russia's stance on the Syrian war or Iran's nuclear program. Russia cannot make itself a richer country or a much larger one, but it has made itself a more important factor in U.S. strategic thinking, and it can use that leverage to extract concessions that matter to it.

If these revisionist powers have gained ground, the status quo powers have been undermined. The deterioration is sharpest in Europe, where the unmitigated disaster of the common currency has divided public opinion and turned the EU's attention in on itself. The EU may have avoided the worst possible consequences of the euro crisis, but both its will and its capacity for effective action beyond its frontiers have been significantly impaired.

The United States has not suffered anything like the economic pain much of Europe has gone through, but with the country facing the foreign policy hangover induced by the Bush-era wars, an increasingly intrusive surveillance state, a slow economic recovery, and an unpopular health-care law, the public mood has soured. On both the left and the right, Americans are questioning the benefits of the current world order and the competence of its architects. Additionally, the public shares the elite consensus that in a post–Cold War world, the United States ought to be able to pay less into the system and get more out. When that doesn't happen, people blame their leaders. In any case, there is little public appetite for large new initiatives at home or abroad, and a cynical public is turning away from a polarized Washington with a mix of boredom and disdain.

Obama came into office planning to cut military spending and reduce the importance of foreign policy in American politics while strengthening the liberal world order. A little more than halfway through his presidency, he finds himself increasingly bogged down in exactly the kinds of geopolitical rivalries he had hoped to transcend. Chinese, Iranian, and Russian revanchism haven't overturned the post–Cold War settlement in Eurasia yet, and may never do so, but they have converted an uncontested status quo into a contested one. U.S. presidents no longer have a free hand as they seek to deepen the liberal system; they are increasingly concerned with shoring up its geopolitical foundations.

THE TWILIGHT OF HISTORY

It was 22 years ago that Fukuyama published The End of History and the Last Man, and it is tempting to see the return of geopolitics as a definitive refutation of his thesis. The reality is more complicated. The end of history, as Fukuyama reminded readers, was Hegel's idea, and even though the revolutionary state had triumphed over the old type of regimes for good, Hegel argued, competition and conflict would continue. He predicted that there would be disturbances in the provinces, even as the heartlands of European civilization moved into a post-historical time. Given that Hegel's provinces included China, India, Japan, and Russia, it should hardly be surprising that more than two centuries later, the disturbances haven't ceased. We are living in the twilight of history rather than at its actual end.

A Hegelian view of the historical process today would hold that substantively little has changed since the beginning of the nineteenth century. To be powerful, states must develop the ideas and institutions that allow them to harness the titanic forces of industrial and informational capitalism. There is no alternative; societies unable or unwilling to embrace this route will end up the subjects of history rather than the makers of it.

But the road to postmodernity remains rocky. In order to increase its power, China, for example, will clearly have to go through a process of economic and political development that will require the country to master the problems that modern Western societies have confronted. There is no assurance, however, that China's path to stable liberal modernity will be any less tumultuous than, say, the one that Germany trod. The twilight of history is not a quiet time.

The second part of Fukuyama's book has received less attention, perhaps because it is less flattering to the West. As Fukuyama investigated what a post-historical society would look like, he made a disturbing discovery. In a world where the great questions have been solved and geopolitics has been subordinated to economics, humanity will look a lot like the nihilistic "last man" described by the philosopher Friedrich Nietzsche: a narcissistic consumer with no greater aspirations beyond the next trip to the mall.

In other words, these people would closely resemble today's European bureaucrats and Washington lobbyists. They are competent enough at managing their affairs among post-historical people, but understanding the motives and countering the strategies of old-fashioned power politicians is hard for them. Unlike their less productive and less stable rivals, post-historical people are unwilling to make sacrifices, focused on the short term, easily distracted, and lacking in courage.

The realities of personal and political life in post-historical societies are very different from those in such countries as China, Iran, and Russia, where the sun of history still shines. It is not just that those different societies bring different personalities and values to the fore; it is also that their institutions work differently and their publics are shaped by different ideas.

Societies filled with Nietzsche's last men (and women) characteristically misunderstand and underestimate their supposedly primitive opponents in supposedly backward societies—a blind spot that could, at least temporarily, offset their countries' other advantages. The tide of history may be flowing inexorably in the direction of liberal capitalist democracy, and the sun of history may indeed be sinking behind the hills. But even as the shadows lengthen and the first of the stars appears, such figures as Putin still stride the world stage. They will not go gentle into that good night, and they will rage, rage against the dying of the light.

WALTER RUSSELL MEAD is James Clarke Chace Professor of Foreign Affairs and Humanities at Bard College and Editor-at-Large of *The American Interest*. Follow him on Twitter **@wrmead**.

The Illusion of Geopolitics

The Enduring Power of the Liberal Order

G. John Ikenberry

Transnational anthem: pro-EU demonstrators singing in Kiev, November 2013.

Walter Russell Mead paints a disturbing portrait of the United States' geopolitical predicament. As he sees it, an increasingly formidable coalition of illiberal powers— China, Iran, and Russia—is determined to undo the post–Cold War settlement and the U.S.-led global order that stands behind it. Across Eurasia, he argues, these aggrieved states are bent on building spheres of influence to threaten the foundations of U.S. leadership and the global order. So the United States must rethink its optimism, including its post–Cold War belief that rising non-Western states can be persuaded to join the West and play by its rules. For Mead, the time has come to confront the threats from these increasingly dangerous geopolitical foes.

But Mead's alarmism is based on a colossal misreading of modern power realities. It is a misreading of the logic and character of the existing world order, which is more stable and expansive than Mead depicts, leading him to overestimate the ability of the "axis of weevils" to undermine it. And it is a misreading of China and Russia, which are not full-scale revisionist powers but part-time spoilers at best, as suspicious of each other as they are of the outside world. True, they look for opportunities to resist the United States' global leadership, and recently, as in the past, they have pushed back against it, particularly when confronted in their own neighborhoods. But even these conflicts are fueled more by weakness—their leaders' and regimes'—than by strength. They have no appealing brand. And when it comes to their overriding interests, Russia and, especially, China are deeply integrated into the world economy and its governing institutions.

Mead also mischaracterizes the thrust of U.S. foreign policy. Since the end of the Cold War, he argues, the United States has ignored geopolitical issues involving territory and spheres of influence and instead adopted a Pollyannaish emphasis on building the global order. But this is a false dichotomy. The United States does not focus on issues of global order, such as arms control and trade, because it assumes that geopolitical conflict is gone forever; it undertakes such efforts precisely because it wants to manage great-power competition. Order building is not premised on the end of geopolitics; it is about how to answer the big questions of geopolitics.

Indeed, the construction of a U.S.-led global order did not begin with the end of the Cold War; it won the Cold War. In the nearly 70 years since World War II, Washington has undertaken sustained efforts to build a far-flung system of multilateral institutions, alliances, trade agreements, and political partnerships. This project has helped draw countries into the United States' orbit. It has helped strengthen global norms and rules that undercut the legitimacy of nineteenth-century-style spheres of influence, bids for regional domination, and territorial grabs. And it has given the United States the capacities, partnerships, and principles to confront today's great-power spoilers and revisionists, such as they are. Alliances, partnerships, multilateralism, democracy— these are the tools of U.S. leadership, and they are winning, not losing, the twenty-first-century struggles over geopolitics and the world order.

THE GENTLE GIANT

In 1904, the English geographer Halford Mackinder wrote that the great power that controlled the heartland of Eurasia would command "the World-Island" and thus the world itself. For Mead, Eurasia has returned as the great prize of geopolitics. Across the far reaches of this supercontinent, he argues, China, Iran, and Russia are seeking to establish their spheres of influence and challenge U.S. interests, slowly but relentlessly attempting to dominate Eurasia and thereby threaten the United States and the rest of the world.

This vision misses a deeper reality. In matters of geopolitics (not to mention demographics, politics, and ideas), the United States has a decisive advantage over China, Iran, and Russia. Although the United States will no doubt come down from the peak of hegemony that it occupied during the unipolar era, its power is still unrivaled. Its wealth and technological advantages remain far out of the reach of China and Russia, to say nothing of Iran. Its recovering economy, now bolstered by massive new natural gas resources, allows it to maintain a global military presence and credible security commitments.

Indeed, Washington enjoys a unique ability to win friends and influence states. According to a study led by the political scientist Brett Ashley Leeds, the United States boasts military partnerships with more than 60 countries, whereas Russia counts eight formal allies and China has just one (North Korea). As one British diplomat told me several years ago, "China doesn't seem to do alliances." But the United States does, and they pay a double dividend: not only do alliances provide a global platform for the projection of U.S. power, but they also distribute the burden of providing security. The military capabilities aggregated in this U.S.-led alliance system outweigh anything China or Russia might generate for decades to come.

Then there are the nuclear weapons. These arms, which the United States, China, and Russia all possess (and Iran is seeking), help the United States in two ways. First, thanks to the logic of mutual assured destruction, they radically reduce the likelihood of great-power war. Such upheavals have provided opportunities for past great powers, including the United States in World War II, to entrench their own international orders. The atomic age has robbed China and Russia of this opportunity. Second, nuclear weapons also make China and Russia more secure, giving them assurance that the United States will never invade. That's a good thing, because it reduces the likelihood that they will resort to desperate moves, born of insecurity, that risk war and undermine the liberal order.

Geography reinforces the United States' other advantages. As the only great power not surrounded by other great powers, the country has appeared less threatening to other states and was able to rise dramatically over the course of the last century without triggering a war. After the Cold War, when the United States was the world's sole superpower, other global powers, oceans away, did not even attempt to balance against it. In fact, the United States' geographic position has led other countries to worry more about abandonment than domination. Allies in Europe, Asia, and the Middle East have sought to draw the United States into playing a greater role in their regions. The result is what the historian Geir Lundestad has called an "empire by invitation."

The United States' geographic advantage is on full display in Asia. Most countries there see China as a greater potential danger—due to its proximity, if nothing else—than the United States. Except for the United States, every major power in the world lives in a crowded geopolitical neighborhood where shifts in power routinely provoke counterbalancing—including by one another. China is discovering this dynamic today as surrounding states react to its rise by modernizing their militaries and reinforcing their alliances. Russia has known it for decades, and has faced it most recently in Ukraine, which in recent years has increased its military spending and sought closer ties to the EU.

Geographic isolation has also given the United States reason to champion universal principles that allow it to access various regions of the world. The country has long promoted the open-door policy and the principle of self-determination and opposed colonialism—less out of a sense of idealism than due to the practical realities of keeping Europe, Asia, and the Middle East open for trade and diplomacy. In the late 1930s, the main question facing the United States was how large a geopolitical space, or "grand area," it would need to exist as a great power in a world of empires, regional blocs, and spheres of influence. World War II made the answer clear: the country's prosperity and security depended on access to every region. And in the ensuing decades, with some important and damaging exceptions, such as Vietnam, the United States has embraced postimperial principles.

It was during these postwar years that geopolitics and order building converged. A liberal international framework was the answer that statesmen such as Dean Acheson, George Kennan, and George Marshall offered to the challenge of Soviet expansionism. The system they built strengthened and enriched the United States and its allies, to the detriment of its illiberal opponents. It also stabilized the world economy and established mechanisms for tackling global problems. The end of the Cold War has not changed the logic behind this project.

Fortunately, the liberal principles that Washington has pushed enjoy near-universal appeal, because they have tended to be a good fit with the modernizing forces of economic growth and social advancement. As the historian Charles Maier has put it, the United States surfed the wave of twentieth-century modernization. But some have argued that this congruence between the American project and the forces of modernity has weakened in recent years. The 2008 financial crisis, the thinking goes, marked a world-historical turning point, at which the United States lost its vanguard role in facilitating economic advancement.

Yet even if that were true, it hardly follows that China and Russia have replaced the United States as the standard-bearers of the global economy. Even Mead does not argue that China, Iran, or Russia offers the world a new model of modernity. If these illiberal powers really do threaten Washington and the rest of the liberal capitalist world, then they will need to find and ride the next great wave of modernization. They are unlikely to do that.

THE RISE OF DEMOCRACY

Mead's vision of a contest over Eurasia between the United States and China, Iran, and Russia misses the more profound power transition under way: the increasing ascendancy of liberal capitalist democracy. To be sure, many liberal democracies are struggling at the moment with slow economic growth, social inequality, and political instability. But the spread of liberal democracy throughout the world, beginning in the late 1970s and accelerating after the Cold War, has dramatically strengthened the United States' position and tightened the geopolitical circle around China and Russia.

It's easy to forget how rare liberal democracy once was. Until the twentieth century, it was confined to the West and parts of Latin America. After World War II, however, it began to reach beyond those realms, as newly independent states established self-rule. During the 1950s, 1960s, and early 1970s, military coups and new dictators put the brakes on democratic transitions. But in the late 1970s, what the political scientist Samuel Huntington termed "the third wave" of democratization washed over southern Europe, Latin America, and East Asia. Then the Cold War ended, and a cohort of former communist states in eastern Europe were brought into the democratic fold. By the late 1990s, 60 percent of all countries had become democracies.

Although some backsliding has occurred, the more significant trend has been the emergence of a group of democratic middle powers, including Australia, Brazil, India, Indonesia, Mexico, South Korea, and Turkey. These rising democracies are acting as stakeholders in the international system: pushing for multilateral cooperation, seeking greater rights and responsibilities, and exercising influence through peaceful means.

Such countries lend the liberal world order new geopolitical heft. As the political scientist Larry Diamond has noted, if Argentina, Brazil, India, Indonesia, South Africa, and Turkey regain their economic footing and strengthen their democratic rule, the G-20, which also includes the United States and European countries, "will have become a strong 'club of democracies,' with only Russia, China, and Saudi Arabia holding out." The rise of a global middle class of democratic states has turned China and Russia into outliers—not, as Mead fears, legitimate contestants for global leadership.

In fact, the democratic upsurge has been deeply problematic for both countries. In eastern Europe, former Soviet states and satellites have gone democratic and joined the West. As worrisome as Russian President Vladimir Putin's moves in Crimea have been, they reflect Russia's geopolitical vulnerability, not its strength. Over the last two decades, the West has crept closer to Russia's borders. In 1999, the Czech Republic, Hungary, and Poland entered NATO. They were joined in 2004 by seven more former members of the Soviet bloc, and in 2009, by Albania and Croatia. In the meantime, six former Soviet republics have headed down the path to membership by joining NATO's Partnership for Peace program. Mead makes much of Putin's achievements in Georgia, Armenia, and Crimea. Yet even though Putin is winning some small battles, he is losing the war. Russia is not on the rise; to the contrary, it is experiencing one of the greatest geopolitical contractions of any major power in the modern era.

Democracy is encircling China, too. In the mid-1980s, India and Japan were the only Asian democracies, but since then, Indonesia, Mongolia, the Philippines, South Korea, Taiwan, and Thailand have joined the club. Myanmar (also called Burma) has made cautious steps toward multiparty rule—steps that have come, as China has not failed to notice, in conjunction with warming relations with the United States. China now lives in a decidedly democratic neighborhood.

These political transformations have put China and Russia on the defensive. Consider the recent developments in Ukraine. The economic and political currents in most of the country are inexorably flowing westward, a trend that terrifies Putin. His only recourse has been to strong-arm Ukraine into resisting the EU and remaining in Russia's orbit. Although he may be able to keep Crimea under Russian control, his grip on the rest of the country is slipping. As the EU diplomat Robert Cooper has noted, Putin can try to delay the moment when Ukraine "affiliates with the EU, but he can't stop it." Indeed, Putin might not even be able to accomplish that, since his provocative moves may serve only to speed Ukraine's move toward Europe.

China faces a similar predicament in Taiwan. Chinese leaders sincerely believe that Taiwan is part of China, but the Taiwanese do not. The democratic transition on the island has made its inhabitants' claims to nationhood more deeply felt and legitimate. A 2011 survey found that if the Taiwanese could be assured that China would not attack Taiwan, 80 percent of them would support declaring independence. Like Russia, China wants geopolitical control over its neighborhood. But the spread of democracy to all corners of Asia has made old-fashioned domination the only way to achieve that, and that option is costly and self-defeating.

While the rise of democratic states makes life more difficult for China and Russia, it makes the world safer for the United States. Those two powers may count as U.S. rivals, but the rivalry takes place on a very uneven playing field: the United States has the most friends, and the most capable ones, too. Washington and its allies account for 75 percent of global military spending. Democratization has put China and Russia in a geopolitical box.

Iran is not surrounded by democracies, but it is threatened by a restive pro-democracy movement at home. More important, Iran is the weakest member of Mead's axis, with a much smaller economy and military than the United States and the other great powers. It is also the target of the strongest international sanctions regime ever assembled, with help from China and Russia. The Obama administration's diplomacy with Iran may or may not succeed, but it is not clear what Mead would do differently to prevent the country from acquiring nuclear weapons. U.S. President Barack Obama's approach has the virtue of offering Tehran a path by which it can move from being a hostile regional power to becoming a more constructive, nonnuclear member of the international community—a potential geopolitical game changer that Mead fails to appreciate.

REVISIONISM REVISITED

Not only does Mead underestimate the strength of the United States and the order it built; he also overstates the degree to which China and Russia are seeking to resist both. (Apart from its nuclear ambitions, Iran looks like a state engaged more in futile protest than actual resistance, so it shouldn't be considered anything close to a revisionist power.) Without a doubt, China and Russia desire greater regional influence. China has made aggressive claims over maritime rights and nearby contested islands, and it has embarked on an arms buildup. Putin has visions of reclaiming Russia's dominance in its "near abroad." Both great powers bristle at U.S. leadership and resist it when they can.

But China and Russia are not true revisionists. As former Israeli Foreign Minister Shlomo Ben-Ami has said, Putin's foreign policy is "more a reflection of his resentment of Russia's geopolitical marginalization than a battle cry from a rising empire." China, of course, is an actual rising power, and this does invite dangerous competition with U.S. allies in Asia. But China is not currently trying to break those alliances or overthrow the wider system of regional security governance embodied in the Association of Southeast Asian Nations and the East Asia Summit. And even if China harbors ambitions of eventually doing so, U.S. security partnerships in the region are, if anything, getting stronger, not weaker. At most, China and Russia are spoilers. They do not have the interests—let alone the ideas, capacities, or allies—to lead them to upend existing global rules and institutions.

In fact, although they resent that the United States stands at the top of the current geopolitical system, they embrace the underlying logic of that framework, and with good reason. Openness gives them access to trade, investment, and technology from other societies. Rules give them tools to protect their sovereignty and interests. Despite controversies over the new idea of "the responsibility to protect" (which has been applied only selectively), the current world order enshrines the age-old norms of state sovereignty and nonintervention. Those Westphalian principles remain the bedrock of world politics—and China and Russia have tied their national interests to them (despite Putin's disturbing irredentism).

It should come as no surprise, then, that China and Russia have become deeply integrated into the existing international order. They are both permanent members of the UN Security Council, with veto rights, and they both participate actively in the World Trade Organization, the International Monetary Fund, the World Bank, and the G-20. They are geopolitical insiders, sitting at all the high tables of global governance.

China, despite its rapid ascent, has no ambitious global agenda; it remains fixated inward, on preserving party rule. Some Chinese intellectuals and political figures, such as Yan Xuetong and Zhu Chenghu, do have a wish list of revisionist goals. They see the Western system as a threat and are waiting for the day when China can reorganize the international order. But these voices do not reach very far into the political elite. Indeed, Chinese leaders have moved away from their earlier calls for sweeping change. In 2007, at its Central Committee meeting, the Chinese Communist Party replaced previous proposals for a "new international economic order" with calls for more modest reforms centering on fairness and justice. The Chinese scholar Wang Jisi has argued that this move is "subtle but important," shifting China's orientation toward that of a global reformer. China now wants a larger role in the International Monetary Fund and the World Bank, greater voice in such forums as the G-20, and wider global use of its currency. That is not the agenda of a country trying to revise the economic order.

China and Russia are also members in good standing of the nuclear club. The centerpiece of the Cold War settlement between the United States and the Soviet Union (and then Russia) was a shared effort to limit atomic weapons. Although U.S.-Russian relations have since soured, the nuclear component of their arrangement has held. In 2010, Moscow and Washington signed the New START treaty, which requires mutual reductions in long-range nuclear weapons.

Before the 1990s, China was a nuclear outsider. Although it had a modest arsenal, it saw itself as a voice of the nonnuclear developing world and criticized arms control agreements and test bans. But in a remarkable shift, China has since come to support the array of nuclear accords, including the Nuclear Nonproliferation Treaty and the Comprehensive Nuclear Test Ban Treaty. It has affirmed a "no first use" doctrine, kept its arsenal small, and taken its entire nuclear force off alert. China has also played an active role in the Nuclear Security Summit, an initiative proposed by Obama in 2009, and it has joined the "P5 process," a collaborate effort to safeguard nuclear weapons.

Across a wide range of issues, China and Russia are acting more like established great powers than revisionist ones. They often choose to shun multilateralism, but so, too, on occasion do the United States and other powerful democracies. (Beijing has ratified the UN Convention on the Law of the Sea; Washington has not.) And China and Russia are using global rules and institutions to advance their own interests. Their struggles with the United States revolve around gaining voice within the existing order and manipulating it to suit their needs. They wish to enhance their positions within the system, but they are not trying to replace it.

HERE TO STAY

Ultimately, even if China and Russia do attempt to contest the basic terms of the current global order, the adventure will be daunting and self-defeating. These powers aren't just up against the United States; they would also have to contend with the most globally organized and deeply entrenched order the world has ever seen, one that is dominated by states that are liberal, capitalist, and democratic. This order is backed by a U.S.-led network of alliances, institutions, geopolitical bargains, client states, and democratic partnerships. It has proved dynamic and expansive, easily integrating rising states, beginning with Japan and Germany after World War II. It has shown a capacity for shared leadership, as exemplified by such forums as the G-8 and the G-20. It has allowed rising non-Western countries to trade and grow, sharing the dividends of modernization. It has accommodated a surprisingly wide variety of political and economic models—social democratic (western Europe), neoliberal (the United Kingdom and the United States), and state capitalist (East Asia). The prosperity of nearly every country—and the stability of its government—fundamentally depends on this order.

In the age of liberal order, revisionist struggles are a fool's errand. Indeed, China and Russia know this. They do not have grand visions of an alternative order. For them, international relations are mainly about the search for commerce and resources, the protection of their sovereignty, and, where possible, regional domination. They have shown no interest in building their own orders or even taking full responsibility for the current one and have offered no alternative visions of global economic or political progress. That's a critical shortcoming, since international orders rise and fall not simply with the power of the leading state; their success also hinges on whether they are seen as legitimate and whether their actual operation solves problems that both weak and powerful states care about. In the struggle for world order, China and Russia (and certainly Iran) are simply not in the game.

Under these circumstances, the United States should not give up its efforts to strengthen the liberal order. The world that Washington inhabits today is one it should welcome. And the grand strategy it should pursue is the one it has followed for decades: deep global engagement. It is a strategy in which the United States ties itself to the regions of the world through trade, alliances, multilateral institutions, and diplomacy. It is a strategy in which the United States establishes leadership not simply through the exercise of power but also through sustained efforts at global problem solving and rule making. It created a world that is friendly to American interests, and it is made friendly because, as President John F. Kennedy once said, it is a world "where the weak are safe and the strong are just."

G. JOHN IKENBERRY is Albert G. Milbank Professor of Politics and International Affairs at Princeton University and George Eastman Visiting Professor at Balliol College, University of Oxford.

The Reform Reformation

International Organizations and the Challenge of Change

Tine Hanrieder

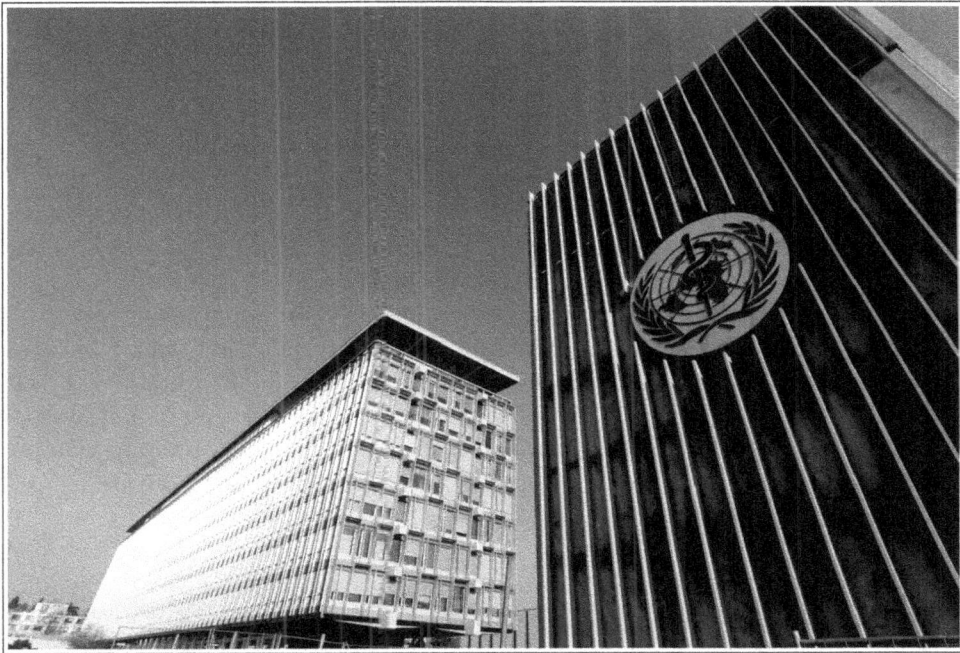

The headquarters of the World Health Organization (WHO) are pictured in Geneva, Switzerland, March 22, 2016.

The system of global governance has changed since the United Nations was established in the 1940s. International organizations have not only become larger, they have also grown in number. Now, these organizations are spun in a complex network that includes states, nongovernmental organizations, and other agencies that operate above the state level.

Even so, international organizations continue to be deeply rooted in the historical events that gave birth to their rise. The World Health Organization (WHO), International Labor Organization, and United Nations Educational, Scientific and Cultural Organization have grown in size and scope and interconnectedness—yet the way in which they operate has not changed much since their founding. In fact, decisions made during each of their formative periods still impact the way in which these organizations enact reforms, govern their field activities, and respond to changes in the system. This is called "path dependence."

But this does not mean that these organizations have not sought to make meaningful reforms in response to a changing world, many of which have been based upon updated ideas about how organizations (and the people within them) should work. So as participating countries, private donors, and even international organization employees themselves place new demands on global organizations, these organizations are seeking new methods to improve the ways in which they function.

THE BUREAUCRACY BUREAU

A main promise during such reforms is to make the organizations less "bureaucratic," since being a bureaucracy is no longer seen as something good. Global organizations try not to appear as impersonal bureaucracies with bloated overhead costs and ineffective operations, but they want to be perceived as dynamic actors that react quickly and effectively to new problems. Yet reform coalitions, which include state representatives as well as new organizational leaders, often claim that the processes international organizations use are labyrinthine and that the sheer size, multitude, and duplication of offices within them cause friction and reduce their impact in the world. As a result, most international organization reforms are accompanied by pledges to "rationalize" their bureaucracies, making them more goal oriented rather than rule driven. Most reform efforts target "efficiency savings" by way of reducing staff, overhead costs, and administrative spending.

As a result, over the past several years, international organizations have dramatically changed the nature of their employees' jobs, as well as the decision-making processes that govern which projects receive funding. In the past, the bureaucratic ideal of the continuity of office meant that employees were expected to act as impersonal cogs—representatives of their organization and of the established procedures and rules of their specific offices, rather than of their own expertise and experience in a given field. This model has since been superseded with a new, more entrepreneurial role for modern bureaucrats—one that is based on the expectation that people work best when they believe they are empowered to be "proactive," mobile, and flexible. This also implies that global organizations increasingly work with short-term consultants instead of civil servants.

Some organizations, such as the WHO, have sought to create a staff of generalists by rotating their employees between their Geneva, Switzerland, headquarters and their regional and field offices. To forestall the risk of overspecialization and compartmentalization, major reforms such as the "One WHO" introduced by former Director-General Gro Harlem Brundtland also involved a massive rotation between departments. And when it comes to decision-making and resource allocation, international organizations are tasked with making smarter, evidence-based decisions on which programs to fund. Many have begun to use computer modeling for planning, to counter the biases inherent in historical routines and political prejudice. For example, in the 1990s, the WHO and the World Bank implemented a measure of the "disability adjusted life years" (DALYs), which was used to determine which public health efforts had the most impact on people's lives. This helped the WHO justify its funding priorities during a period of major reform. Other organizations have developed comparable techniques of evidence-based decision-making for the planning, implementation, and, if needed, adaptation of their operations.

A UNESCO World Heritage emblem outside the Potala Palace in Lhasa, Tibet Autonomous Region, China, November 17, 2015.

THE MORE THINGS CHANGE

Ironically, however, reform efforts themselves tend to become bureaucratized, even if their aim is to overcome inefficient bureaucratic cultures. The diffusion of the new bureaucratic "culture of change" can be observed at all levels of international organization reform, ranging from program formulation to human resource management. Organizations seek to replace routines with initiatives, continuity with flexibility, and rules with results. But in the process, these organizational efforts become highly formalized in their own right and, worse yet, can create more administrative bloat rather than less.

For example, when former UN Secretary-General Kofi Annan's reform efforts led to the creation of a Strategic Planning Unit, another layer of bureaucracy was born. The same could be said for Brundtland's WHO reorganization efforts, which created the Evidence for Information and Policy Cluster. In fact, the One WHO reforms did not lead to a reduction of staff; rather, it caused an increase in headquarter posts for both short-term and permanent employees.

Similarly, the implementation of so-called results-based management that was brought to the UN by Annan often means formalizing budgeting procedures that were once resource based. In this process, international organization employees need to spend considerable time on formulating strategic objectives, performance indicators, and scorecards. The managerialism that is meant to reduce overhead thus produces its own overhead. In other words, strategy making entails bureaucracy making, and this again creates the need for "rationalization." Or, in the words of Stockholm School of Economics Professor Emeritus Nils Brunsson and University of Bergen Professor Emeritus Johan Olsen, "Reforms tend to generate reforms."

MAKING A REAL DIFFERENCE

Institutional leaders, together with the states that support them, should rethink the way in which they approach reform efforts if they wish to enact meaningful change in their organizations. Past reform efforts paint a grim picture. Even if few reform efforts have ever failed completely, many goals have never been attained, and new problems have been created through these very reforms themselves. In such situations, diversions are very tempting for those who are pressed to provide results to their stakeholders, who pursue smaller and "meta-level" managerial goals, which then come at the sacrifice of larger aims. Only hindsight can reveal whether reforms have been worth undertaking. And the dilemma that reformers should not overpromise on the one hand, but avoid sacrificing bigger efforts for the low-hanging fruit—such as attaining some formal indicators or implementing new managerial techniques—on the other, is difficult to deal with.

However, some traps can and should be avoided if international organizations want to pursue meaningful reform. Reformers should resist the temptation to micromanage. Inventing a stream of intermediate goals may give the illusion of control, but this method also creates additional red tape. This also applies to the tendency of donor states and private donors to tightly "earmark" their contributions for very specific activities, a practice that has become paralyzing. Earmarks often make it impossible for organizations to allocate resources properly, undermining their results-based budgeting policies. Worse yet, earmarks often make organizations sit on unspent money, since restricted donations can be used only for very specific purposes. For example, some earmarks authorize departments only to buy equipment but do not finance a staff of personnel to handle it. Greater flexibility here could impinge on day-to-day financial oversight for donors but could help organizations become more efficient with their budgets. Reformers should also give up the illusion that "efficiency savings" can fix all of their problems. The WHO has encountered emergency situations as a result of overhead cuts, leading donors to finance the organization's administrative budget to cover core running costs. Likewise, the outsourcing of certain services to low-wage countries may cut spending at first but slows down many activities and later on creates follow-up costs.

Finally, reformers must tackle the historical privileges that some departments enjoy within international organizations. These departments are often able to halt or even block reforms owing to their historical stature. It is here that history begets reform efforts—an overarching issue plaguing international organizations as they adapt to the challenges of the twenty-first century. To move ahead, groups must shed themselves of the ineffective policies of the past. The road ahead may be uncertain, but adhering to old models of reform proves that new efforts are needed. Now, it's up to them to forge a way forward.

TINE HANRIEDER is a Global Governance Research Fellow at the WZB Berlin Social Science Center. She is the author of International Organization in Time: Fragmentation and Reform (Oxford, 2015).

The End of the G-20

Has the Group Outlived Its Purpose?

Rebecca Liao

China's President Xi Jinping attends a news conference after the closing of G20 Summit in Hangzhou, Zhejiang Province, China, September 5, 2016.

Over Labor Day weekend, the leaders of the G-20 countries gathered in Hangzhou, China, for their annual summit. Their goal this year: save the good name of globalization, which has recently taken a beating. In the wake of Brexit, the U.S. Republican presidential candidacy of Donald Trump, the rise of the European far right, and China's own anti-Westernism, the G-20 leaders were supposed to renew their commitment to collective economic growth and open cross-border trade and investment. Trouble is, few of the member countries, including China, are interested in promoting these goals in the short term. The United States' stance on trade is growing increasingly protectionist. Both presidential candidates oppose the Trans-

Pacific Partnership trade agreement on grounds that U.S. workers and industry will come out on the losing end. Chinese investment destinations such as Germany, the United Kingdom, the United States, and Africa are refusing ever more high-profile cross-border deals with Chinese companies, due to purported national security concerns. For its own part, China feels that it is not in a position given the slowdown of its own economy to champion outward-facing policies. It is ironic, given China's nearly gaffe-free, luxurious turn as host of the G-20, capped off by a communiqué promising all the right solutions to global problems, that the most important outcome of this summit is that it made abundantly clear that the world needs to reevaluate the organization's role. The sort of domestic policy coordination that it regards as a holy grail has severe limits when tested by political and economic realities on the ground. After two days of meetings, and a year's worth of side meetings between finance ministers and other officials, the Paris Climate Agreement was the only initiative with concrete requirements on which the G-20 could agree. That is a powerful signal that other issues previously imagined as global in nature are in fact not.

Leaders pose for a family picture during the G20 Summit in Hangzhou, Zhejiang province, China September 4, 2016.

FORGED IN CRISIS The tradition of the G-20 summit was established in late 2008 as a response to the financial crisis and in recognition that emerging economic powers outside the G-7 would be instrumental to restabilizing the global financial system. At a summit in November 2008, the G-20 leaders agreed to contribute

$1.1 trillion to the IMF and the World Bank, among other international financial organizations. That money would in turn be used for capital infusions to countries in times of economic distress, preventing more wide-scale contagion. The countries also agreed to stricter regulation of financial institutions, including hedge funds. Most surprising, and perhaps as a sign of the pressure the leaders felt to act in the face of the 2008 crisis, they committed to cooperating on international measures against tax evasion, an initiative that would mean ceding some sovereignty over domestic revenue generation policies. For their part of the $1.1 trillion contribution, the new emerging market contingent of the G-20 did not leave empty-handed. Of the total amount raised, $43 billion came from China. In addition, Beijing agreed to pass a fiscal stimulus package of $586 billion. Brazil, Russia, India, and South Africa also figured prominently in the IMF's capital campaign. At the Pittsburgh summit in 2009, the G-20 leaders agreed to increase developing countries' voting power in the IMF by five percent and the World Bank by three percent. China would then vault over Germany, the United Kingdom, and France to hold the third-largest contingent of shares and voting power at the IMF and World Bank. This acknowledgment of China's emergence as a global leader has led to other significant achievements for Beijing as well: the yuan is now part of the IMF's currency basket, and a heavy campaign is underway to make sure China gains market economy status at the WTO early next year. Hosting the G-20 summit for the first time was but the latest manifestation of China's newfound stature. The G-20's efforts in the immediate aftermath of the 2008 financial crisis have been generally praised. For those who dreamed of full cooperation and coordination between countries to unlock the full potential of globalization, the hope was that initiatives along the same vein would continue. Without the pressure of disaster, however, the G-20 reverted to its mode of operation prior to 2008. Instead of coordinating economic policy among the world's wealthiest countries, it broadened its scope to include climate change, investment initiatives, and human rights. Since its members are largely unable to come to a meaningful consensus on this expanded range of issues, the G-20 then became a think tank of sorts. In conjunction with other multilateral organizations such as the IMF and the Organization for Economic Cooperation and Development, the G-20 produces reports and scholarship on policy prescriptions that will hopefully inform the leaders' actions at the summits and other side meetings.

Performers give a performance during an evening gala for the G20 Summit at West Lake in Hangzhou, Zhejiang province, China, September 4, 2016.

GROWING PAINS Come 2014, however, the G-20 countries became concerned about the slow speed of recovery after the 2008 financial crisis. At the summit in Brisbane, Australia, that year, the leaders agreed to target a global 2.1 percent growth rate by 2018. According to IMF and OECD projections, a quarter of this increase would be attributable to positive externalities from the G-20 countries implementing the agreed-upon growth measures at the same time. These policies included: greater investment in infrastructure projects, fostering competition, reducing the barriers to trade and doing business abroad, and creating jobs, particularly for young people. Two years later, the IMF expressed concern that the G-20 was on track to fall short of its target, particularly because the growth rates of advanced industrial economies remained low. In addition to changing demographics and low productivity, the IMF blamed low growth in these countries on a lack of investment. Leading up to this year's summit, the general understanding was that in order to save the project of globalization, growth rates would have to be increased so that populations would no longer use it as a scapegoat. It became all the more urgent, then, to get back on track for the Brisbane summit's 2.1 percent growth target. This year's summit layered on additional commitments aimed at promoting collective growth. Chief among them was promoting innovation. The countries promised greater openness in their economies, geared toward fostering a friendly environment for the so-called new industrial revolution. The digital economy in each country would receive support through exchange of human capital, cross-border partnerships, and capital investments. Developing economies would receive special attention in crossing the digital divide. Interestingly, the communiqué included little about cybersecurity or the need to protect intellectual property rights on an international level. On the other hand, voluntary transfers of technology would be encouraged. The countries also agreed to pursue structural reforms to boost economic efficiency. As ever, countries would do their utmost to resist trade protectionism and overly restrictive capital controls. Prior to the summit, US Treasury Secretary Jack Lew announced that he had brokered a deal among the G-20 countries to adopt expansive monetary and fiscal policy rather than austerity in service of global growth. Canada, China, South Korea, Japan, and other countries in Europe would accordingly pass measures later this year to delay tax increases or increase their government spending. Despite meeting in the shadow of crisis again, the G-20 will likely find that few of the growth measures they set forth in 2014 and this year will have been implemented, and certainly not in a coordinated fashion among the member countries. The initiatives that they now seek to undertake are quite different from a one-time cash infusion made possible by short-term expansive monetary policy, or even from green initiatives to combat climate change. Those were responses to actual global problems, where the consequences are widely acknowledged to be borderless in nature, and risks can be significantly reduced with international cooperation. Methods for growth, on the other hand, are generally the purview of domestic policy. The end result is that even though countries may pledge to coordinate, political and economic realities at home mean that national interests come first. Indeed, the voice of China as the host nation could be heard in this year's G-20 communiqué with its repeated variations on the phrase "according to national circumstances." For example, structural reforms mean growing pains as those who are entrenched in the current institutional framework will be displaced. In China's case, an economic slowdown is therefore not the best time to implement these on a strict timetable or according to international mandates when local conditions may call for different solutions. Walls have gone up for cross-border investment in the last year as countries become increasingly wary about foreign ownership of prized national assets. Technological innovation is also a largely domestic project in which the national security implications are growing increasingly sensitive. Even consumer technology companies can be said to have security risks that do not merit their being able to freely operate or purchase companies overseas. Finally, the fate of protectionism remains to be seen. If the political mood does not significantly change in Western industrialized nations by the end of the year, trade openness will suffer. Again, countries make this calculation for themselves, not because they don't understand the intuition behind free trade and comparative advantage. Rather, there is good evidence that countries can yield short-term gains from fostering home industries. MISSING THE BIGGER PICTURE The larger concern is not that the G-20, or any multilateral organization, is ill equipped to coordinate domestic agendas for growth but that the G-20 members still accept the orthodoxy that all growth is good. Discontent leading to anti-globalization does not come from lack of growth so much as from inequality. Although economic openness has directed a share of the wealth to developing countries and narrowed the gap between them and the

Western industrialized world, inequality within countries has increased. The solutions to this problem are almost exclusively domestic: greater investment in education, job retraining, more aggressive tax-and-transfer programs, and the like. One area in which international cooperation is crucial, however, is in tax regulations that prevent tax evasion. High-net-worth individuals and corporations are able to move their income to jurisdictions with lower taxes, most of the time through legal means. This ability to hide income stymies tax-and-transfer programs, not to mention that it has meant a significant hit to government revenues in advanced and developing countries alike. In response, the G-20 and OECD have partnered to devise and implement a framework on tax reform that individual countries may implement at a customized pace. The success of this initiative remains to be seen since it internationalizes a tool that is at the heart of a country's economic sovereignty. Asking countries to incrementally but broadly give up that sovereignty is not a worthwhile endeavor for the G-20, or for any multilateral organization. It would be better served by focusing on problems that are recognized to be global in nature and by encouraging countries to cooperate on other economic issues without standardizing growth initiatives or imposing growth targets. In the end, after the summits are over, the job of saving globalization is still waiting for the leaders when they arrive home.

REBECCA LIAO is the Director of Business Development at Globality, Inc. She is also a writer and China analyst.

Will the Liberal Order Survive?

The History of an Idea

Joseph S. Nye Jr.

Called to order: Barack Obama chairing a UN Security Council meeting, September 2009

During the nineteenth century, the United States played a minor role in the global balance of power. The country did not maintain a large standing army, and as late as the 1870s, the U.S. Navy was smaller than the navy of Chile. Americans had no problems using force to acquire land or resources (as Mexico and the Native American nations could attest), but for the most part, both the U.S. government and the American public opposed significant involvement in international affairs outside the Western Hemisphere.

A flirtation with imperialism at the end of the century drew U.S. attention outward, as did the growing U.S. role in the world economy, paving the way for President Woodrow Wilson to take the United States into World War I. But the costs of the war and the failure of Wilson's ambitious attempt to reform international politics afterward turned U.S. attention inward once again during the 1920s and 1930s, leading to the strange situation of an increasingly great power holding itself aloof from an increasingly turbulent world.

Like their counterparts elsewhere, U.S. policymakers sought to advance their country's national interests, usually in straightforward, narrowly defined ways. They saw international politics and economics as an intense competition among states constantly jockeying for position and advantage. When the Great Depression hit, therefore, U.S. officials, like others, raced to protect their domestic economy as quickly and fully as possible, adopting beggar-thy-neighbor tariffs and deepening the crisis in the process. And a few years later, when aggressive dictatorships emerged and threatened peace, they and their counterparts in Europe and elsewhere did something similar in the security sphere, trying to ignore the growing dangers, pass the buck, or defer conflict through appeasement.

By this point, the United States had become the world's strongest power, but it saw no value in devoting resources or attention to providing global public goods such as an open economy or international security. There was no U.S.-led liberal order in the 1930s, and the result was a "low dishonest decade," in the words of W. H. Auden, of depression, tyranny, war, and genocide.

With their countries drawn into the conflagration despite their efforts to avoid it, Western officials spent the first half of the 1940s trying to defeat the Axis powers while working to construct a different and better world for afterward. Rather than continue to see economic and security issues as solely national concerns, they now sought to cooperate with one another, devising a rules-based system that in theory would allow like-minded nations to enjoy peace and prosperity in common.

The liberal international order that emerged after 1945 was a loose array of multilateral institutions in which the United States provided global public goods such as freer trade and freedom of the seas and weaker states were given institutional access to the exercise of U.S. power. The Bretton Woods institutions were set up while the war was still in progress. When other countries proved too poor or weak to fend for themselves afterward, the Truman administration decided to break with U.S. tradition and make open-ended alliances, provide substantial aid to other countries, and deploy U.S. military forces abroad. Washington gave the United Kingdom a major loan in 1946, took responsibility for supporting pro-Western governments in Greece and Turkey in 1947, invested heavily in European recovery with the Marshall Plan in 1948, created NATO in 1949, led a military coalition to protect South Korea from invasion in 1950, and signed a new security treaty with Japan in 1960.

These and other actions both bolstered the order and contained Soviet power. As the American diplomat George Kennan and others noted, there were five crucial areas of industrial productivity and strength in the postwar world: the United States, the Soviet Union, the United Kingdom, continental Europe, and Northeast Asia. To protect itself and prevent a third world war, Washington chose to isolate the Soviet Union and bind itself tightly to the other three, and U.S. troops remain in Europe, Asia, and elsewhere to this day. And within this framework, global economic, social, and ecological interdependence grew. By 1970, economic globalization had recovered to the level it had reached before being disrupted by World War I in 1914.

The mythology that has grown up around the order can be exaggerated. Washington may have displayed a general preference for democracy and openness, but it frequently supported dictators or made cynical self-interested moves along the way. In its first decades, the postwar system was largely limited to a group of like-minded states centered on the Atlantic littoral; it did not include many large countries such as China, India, and the Soviet bloc states, and it did not always have benign effects on nonmembers. In global military terms, the United States was not hegemonic, because the Soviet Union balanced U.S. power. And even when its power was greatest, Washington could not prevent the "loss" of China, the partition of Germany and Berlin, a draw in Korea, Soviet suppression of insurrections within its own bloc, the creation and survival of a communist regime in Cuba, and failure in Vietnam.

Americans have had bitter debates and partisan differences over military interventions and other foreign policy issues over the years, and they have often grumbled about paying for the defense of other rich countries. Still, the demonstrable success of the order in helping secure and stabilize the world over the past seven decades has led to a strong consensus that defending, deepening, and extending this system has been and continues to be the central task of U.S. foreign policy.

Churchill, Roosevelt, and Stalin and the Yalta Conference, 1945

Until now, that is—for recently, the desirability and sustainability of the order have been called into question as never before. Some critics, such as U.S. President-elect Donald Trump, have argued that the costs of maintaining the order outweigh its benefits and that Washington would be better off handling its interactions with other countries on a case-by-case transactional basis, making sure it "wins" rather than "loses" on each deal or commitment. Others claim that the foundations of the order are eroding because of a long-term global power transition involving the dramatic rise of Asian economies such as China and India. And still others see it as threatened by a broader diffusion of power from governments to nonstate actors thanks to ongoing changes in politics, society, and technology. The order, in short, is facing its greatest challenges in generations. Can it survive, and will it?

POWER CHALLENGED AND DIFFUSED

Public goods are benefits that apply to everyone and are denied to no one. At the national level, governments provide many of these to their citizens: safety for people and property, economic infrastructure, a clean environment. In the absence of international government, global public goods—a clean climate or financial stability or freedom of the seas—have sometimes been provided by coalitions led by the largest power, which benefits the most from these goods and can afford to pay for them. When the strongest powers fail to appreciate this dynamic, global public goods are underproduced and everybody suffers.

The mythology that has grown up around the order can be exaggerated.

Some observers see the main threat to the current liberal order coming from the rapid rise of a China that does not always appear to appreciate that great power carries with it great responsibilities. They worry that China is about to pass the United States in power and that when it does, it will not uphold the current order because it views it as an external imposition reflecting others' interests more than its own. This concern is misguided, however, for two reasons: because China is unlikely to surpass the United States in power anytime soon and because it understands and appreciates the order more than is commonly realized.

Contrary to the current conventional wisdom, China is not about to replace the United States as the world's dominant country. Power involves the ability to get what you want from others, and it can involve payment, coercion, or attraction. China's economy has grown dramatically in recent decades, but it is still only 61 percent of the size of the U.S. economy, and its rate of growth is slowing. And even if China does surpass the United States in total economic size some decades from now, economic might is just part of the geopolitical equation. According to the International Institute for Strategic Studies, the United States spends four times as much on its military as does China, and although Chinese capabilities have been increasing in recent years, serious observers think that China will not be able to exclude the United States from the western Pacific, much less exercise global military hegemony. And as for soft power, the ability to attract others, a recent index published by Portland, a London consultancy, ranks the United States first and China 28th. And as China tries to catch up, the United States will not be standing still. It has favorable demographics, increasingly cheap energy, and the world's leading universities and technology companies.

Moreover, China benefits from and appreciates the existing international order more than it sometimes acknowledges. It is one of only five countries with a veto in the UN Security Council and has gained from liberal economic institutions, such as the World Trade Organization (where it accepts dispute-settlement judgments that go against it) and the International Monetary Fund (where its voting rights have increased and it fills an important deputy director position). China is now the second-largest funder of UN peacekeeping forces and has participated in UN programs related to Ebola and climate change. In 2015, Beijing joined with

Washington in developing new norms for dealing with climate change and conflicts in cyberspace. On balance, China has tried not to overthrow the current order but rather to increase its influence within it.

The order is facing its greatest challenges in generations.

The order will inevitably look somewhat different as the twenty-first century progresses. China, India, and other economies will continue to grow, and the U.S. share of the world economy will drop. But no other country, including China, is poised to displace the United States from its dominant position. Even so, the order may still be threatened by a general diffusion of power away from governments toward nonstate actors. The information revolution is putting a number of transnational issues, such as financial stability, climate change, terrorism, pandemics, and cybersecurity, on the global agenda at the same time as it is weakening the ability of all governments to respond.

Complexity is growing, and world politics will soon not be the sole province of governments. Individuals and private organizations—from corporations and nongovernmental organizations to terrorists and social movements—are being empowered, and informal networks will undercut the monopoly on power of traditional bureaucracies. Governments will continue to possess power and resources, but the stage on which they play will become ever more crowded, and they will have less ability to direct the action.

Even if the United States remains the largest power, accordingly, it will not be able to achieve many of its international goals acting alone. For example, international financial stability is vital to the prosperity of Americans, but the United States needs the cooperation of others to ensure it. Global climate change and rising sea levels will affect the quality of life, but Americans cannot manage these problems by themselves. And in a world where borders are becoming more porous, letting in everything from drugs to infectious diseases to terrorism, nations must use soft power to develop networks and build institutions to address shared threats and challenges.

China is unlikely to surpass the United States in power anytime soon.

Washington can provide some important global public goods largely by itself. The U.S. Navy is crucial when it comes to policing the law of the seas and defending freedom of navigation, and the U.S. Federal Reserve undergirds international financial stability by serving as a lender of last resort. On the new transnational issues, however, success will require the cooperation of others—and thus empowering others can help the United States accomplish its own goals. In this sense, power becomes a positive-sum game: one needs to think of not just the United States' power over others but also the power to solve problems that the United States can acquire by working with others. In such a world, the ability to connect with others becomes a major source of power, and here, too, the United States leads the pack. The United States comes first in the Lowy Institute's ranking of nations by number of embassies, consulates, and missions. It has some 60 treaty allies, and The Economist estimates that nearly 100 of the 150 largest countries lean toward it, while only 21 lean against it.

Increasingly, however, the openness that enables the United States to build networks, maintain institutions, and sustain alliances is itself under siege. This is why the most important challenge to the provision of world order in the twenty-first century comes not from without but from within.

POPULISM VS. GLOBALIZATION

Even if the United States continues to possess more military, economic, and soft-power resources than any other country, it may choose not to use those resources to provide public goods for the international system at large. It did so during the interwar years, after all, and in the wake of the conflicts in Afghanistan and Iraq, a 2013 poll found that 52 percent of Americans believed that "the U.S. should mind its own business internationally and let other countries get along the best they can on their own."

The 2016 presidential election was marked by populist reactions to globalization and trade agreements in both major parties, and the liberal international order is a project of just the sort of cosmopolitan elites whom populists see as the enemy. The roots of populist reactions are both economic and cultural. Areas that have lost jobs to foreign competition appear to have tended to support Trump, but so did older white males who have lost status with the rise in power of other demographic groups. The U.S. Census Bureau projects that in less than three decades, whites will no longer be a racial majority in the United States, precipitating the anxiety and fear that contributed to Trump's appeal, and such trends suggest that populist passions will outlast Trump's campaign.

It has become almost conventional wisdom to argue that the populist surge in the United States, Europe, and elsewhere marks the beginning of the end of the contemporary era of globalization and that turbulence may follow in its wake, as happened after the end of an earlier period of globalization a century ago. But circumstances are so different today that the analogy doesn't hold up. There are so many buffers against turbulence now, at both the domestic and the international level, that a descent into economic and geopolitical chaos, as in the 1930s, is not in the cards. Discontent and frustration are likely to continue, and the election of Trump and the British vote to leave the EU demonstrate that populist reactions are common to many

Western democracies. Policy elites who want to support globalization and an open economy will clearly need to pay more attention to economic inequality, help those disrupted by change, and stimulate broad-based economic growth.

It would be a mistake to read too much about long-term trends in U.S. public opinion from the heated rhetoric of the recent election. The prospects for elaborate trade agreements such as the Trans-Pacific Partnership and the Transatlantic Trade and Investment Partnership have suffered, but there is not likely to be a reversion to protectionism on the scale of the 1930s. A June 2016 poll by the Chicago Council on Global Affairs, for example, found that 65 percent of Americans thought that globalization was mostly good for the United States, despite concerns about a loss of jobs. And campaign rhetoric notwithstanding, in a 2015 Pew survey, 51 percent of respondents said that immigrants strengthened the country.

World politics will soon not be the sole province of governments.

Nor will the United States lose the ability to afford to sustain the order. Washington currently spends less than four percent of its GDP on defense and foreign affairs. That is less than half the share that it spent at the height of the Cold War. Alliances are not significant economic burdens, and in some cases, such as that of Japan, it is cheaper to station troops overseas than at home. The problem is not guns versus butter but guns versus butter versus taxes. Because of a desire to avoid raising taxes or further increasing the national debt, the U.S. national security budget is currently locked in a zero-sum tradeoff with domestic expenditures on education, infrastructure, and research and development. Politics, not absolute economic constraints, will determine how much is spent on what.

The disappointing track record of recent U.S. military interventions has also undermined domestic support for an engaged global role. In an age of transnational terrorism and refugee crises, keeping aloof from all intervention in the domestic affairs of other countries is neither possible nor desirable. But regions such as the Middle East are likely to experience turmoil for decades, and Washington will need to be more careful about the tasks it takes on. Invasion and occupation breed resentment and opposition, which in turn raise the costs of intervention while lowering the odds of success, further undermining public support for an engaged foreign policy.

Political fragmentation and demagoguery, finally, pose yet another challenge to the United States' ability to provide responsible international leadership, and the 2016 election revealed just how fragmented the American electorate is. The U.S. Senate, for example, has failed to ratify the UN Convention on the Law of the Sea, despite the fact that the country is relying on it to help protect freedom of navigation in the South China Sea against Chinese provocations. Congress failed for five years to fulfill an important U.S. commitment to support the reallocation of International Monetary Fund quotas from Europe to China, even though it would have cost almost nothing to do so. Congress has passed laws violating the international legal principle of sovereign immunity, a principle that protects not just foreign governments but also American diplomatic and military personnel abroad. And domestic resistance to putting a price on carbon emissions makes it hard for the United States to lead the fight against climate change.

The United States will remain the world's leading military power for decades to come, and military force will remain an important component of U.S. power. A rising China and a declining Russia frighten their neighbors, and U.S. security guarantees in Asia and Europe provide critical reassurance for the stability that underlies the prosperity of the liberal order. Markets depend on a framework of security, and maintaining alliances is an important source of influence for the United States.

At the same time, military force is a blunt instrument unsuited to dealing with many situations. Trying to control the domestic politics of nationalist foreign populations is a recipe for failure, and force has little to offer in addressing issues such as climate change, financial stability, or Internet governance. Maintaining networks, working with other countries and international institutions, and helping establish norms to deal with new transnational issues are crucial. It is a mistake to equate globalization with trade agreements. Even if economic globalization were to slow, technology is creating ecological, political, and social globalization that will all require cooperative responses.

Leadership is not the same as domination, and Washington's role in helping stabilize the world and underwrite its continued progress may be even more important now than ever. Americans and others may not notice the security and prosperity that the liberal order provides until they are gone—but by then, it may be too late.

JOSEPH S. NYE JR. is University Distinguished Service Professor at the Harvard Kennedy School of Government and the author of *Is the American Century Over?*

Liberalism in Retreat

The Demise of a Dream

Robin Niblett

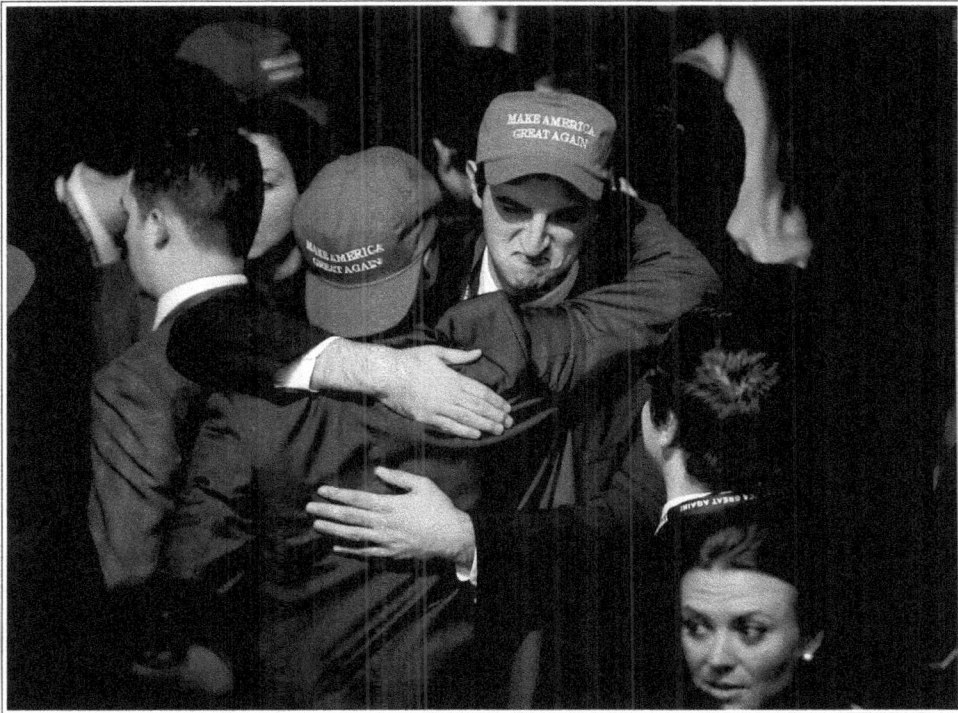

America First: Trump supporters on election night, November 8, 2016.

The liberal international order has always depended on the idea of progress. Since 1945, Western policymakers have believed that open markets, democracy, and individual human rights would gradually spread across the entire globe. Today, such hopes seem naive.

In Asia, the rise of China threatens to challenge U.S. military and economic hegemony, as Beijing seeks to draw American allies such as the Philippines and Thailand into its political orbit. In the Middle East, the United States and its European allies have failed to guide the region toward a more liberal and peaceful future in the wake of the Arab Spring and have proved powerless to halt the conflict in Syria. Russia's geopolitical influence has reached heights unseen since the Cold War, as the country attempts to roll back liberal advances on its periphery.

But the more important threats to the order are internal. For over 50 years, the European Union has seemed to represent the advance guard of a new liberalism in which nations pool sovereignty and cooperate ever more closely with one another. But today, as it reels from one crisis to the next, the EU has stopped expanding. After the British vote to leave the bloc last June, it will probably shrink for the first time in its history.

Across the ocean, the U.S. commitment to global leadership, which until now has sustained the order through good times and bad, looks weaker than at any point since World War II. The Republican president-elect Donald Trump ran on an explicitly "America First" platform, pledged to renegotiate U.S. trade deals, praised Russian President Vladimir Putin, and called into question U.S. commitments to NATO. Meanwhile, President Barack Obama's "rebalance" to Asia has struggled to take off. Beijing has wasted no time in laying out its own vision for a more integrated Eurasia that may exclude the United States and in which China will play the leading role.

Over the past half century, as other political systems have crumbled, the liberal international order has risen to face its challenges. Yet so long as the economies of its leading members remain fragile and their political institutions divided, the order that they have championed is unlikely to regain the political momentum that helped democracy spread across the globe. Instead, it will evolve into a less ambitious project: a liberal international economic order that encompasses states with diverse domestic political systems. In the short term, this will allow democracies and their illiberal counterparts to find ways to coexist. In the longer term, providing it can adapt, liberal democracy is likely to regain its supremacy.

LIBERALISM ON TOP

In the aftermath of World War II, Western policymakers, especially in the United States and the United Kingdom, set out to build a global system that would ensure that they would never repeat the disastrous failures of international cooperation of the interwar period. The architects of the system sought to promote not just economic development and individual fulfillment but also world peace. The best hope for that, they contended, lay in free markets, individual rights, the rule of law, and elected governments, which would be checked by independent judiciaries, free presses, and vibrant civil societies.

Over the past half century, as other political systems have crumbled, the liberal international order has risen to face its challenges.

At the heart of the order were the Bretton Woods institutions—the International Monetary Fund and the World Bank—and the General Agreement on Tariffs and Trade, which became the World Trade Organization in 1995. Underpinning all these institutions was the belief that open and transparent markets with minimal government intervention—the so-called Washington consensus—would lay the foundation for economic growth. Guided by these principles, U.S. economic, military, and diplomatic support helped Germany and the other nations of Western Europe, as well as Japan, recover from the destruction of World War II.

Western policymakers were confident that transitions to open markets would inevitably lead to the spread of democracy. On many occasions, they were proved right. Liberal democracy has gradually expanded across Europe, Asia, Latin America, and sub-Saharan Africa, especially since the end of the Cold War. According to the U.S. nonprofit Freedom House, the number of democratic governments increased from 44 in 1997 to 86 in 2015, accounting for about 68 percent of global GDP and 40 percent of the world's population.

As the order expanded, a new liberal idea gained ground: that governments that mistreat their populations and foment instability in their neighborhoods forfeit their sovereign right to rule. The International Criminal Court, which encroaches on sovereignty in the name of justice, was established in 1998. One year later, British Prime Minister Tony Blair laid out his doctrine of liberal interventionism in Chicago, declaring that, in a world of growing interdependence, "the principle of non-interference must be qualified in some important respects." In 2005, the UN General Assembly endorsed the "responsibility to protect," the concept that when a state fails to prevent atrocities, foreign governments can intervene to do so. In an ascendant liberal international order, the fundamental Westphalian principle that sovereign governments have the right to control their internal affairs—the principle that underlies international law and the UN—increasingly depended on governments' adhering to Western standards of human rights. The liberal order seemed to be setting the rules for the entire international community.

THINGS FALL APART

But over the past decade, buffeted by financial crises, populist insurgencies, and the resurgence of authoritarian powers, the liberal international order has stumbled.

According to the political scientist Larry Diamond, since 2006, the world has entered a "democratic recession": the spread of individual freedom and democracy has come to a halt, if not retreated.

The greatest danger comes from within. The system's leading powers are facing sustained domestic political and economic uncertainty. More than 25 years of stagnant median wages in the United States and parts of Europe have eroded the credibility of elites and the appeal of globalization. The opening up of economies to ever more trade, investment, and immigration has increased total national wealth, but it has not translated into local gains for large segments of society. The lax financial regulation that preceded the 2008 financial crisis and the bank bailouts that followed it have shattered people's faith in government, and the Great Recession undermined their support for open capital markets, which seemed to benefit only a narrow global elite.

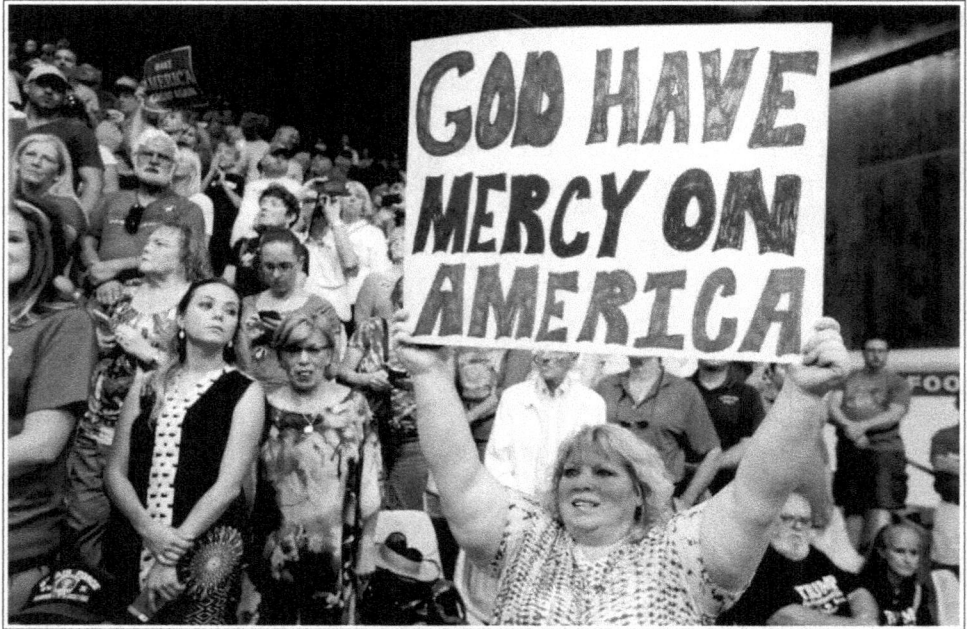

A supporter holds up a sign as Republican presidential nominee Donald Trump speaks during a campaign rally in Sarasota, Florida, November 2016.

Trump's victory, the decision by a majority of British voters to leave the EU, and the rise of populist parties in both the prosperous north and the poorer south of Europe represent visible symptoms of this deep unease with globalization. So, too, does the collapse in popular support in the United States and the EU for expanding international trade, whether through the Trans-Pacific Partnership in the United States or the Transatlantic Trade and Investment Partnership in Europe. In a 2014 Pew Research survey, 87 percent of respondents in developing economies agreed that trade benefits the economy, whereas around half of all respondents in France, Italy, and the United States said they believed that trade destroys jobs and lowers wages.

Across Europe, resistance to deeper political integration has grown. For the past 60 years, the willingness of the EU's member states to pool their sovereign power in supranational legal structures provided a benchmark for other countries that sought to cooperate more closely in their regions. As the political scientist Simon Serfaty put it in 2003, Europeans had transformed their systems of political governance from city-states to nation-states to member states. Now, this process has ground to a halt—and it may well reverse.

The British vote to leave the EU will likely prove an outlier: the United Kingdom joined the European Economic Community, the EU's predecessor, only in 1973, 16 years after its founding; the United Kingdom has a long history of Euroskepticism; and it opted out of the single currency and the Schengen area of open borders. Other countries will probably not follow the United Kingdom out of the EU. But few European leaders appear willing to continue relinquishing their countries' sovereignty. Many European states have rejected EU requests that they accept a quota of refugees. The richer members of the eurozone are refusing to pool their financial resources in a common deposit insurance scheme to ensure the long-term viability of the single currency. Today, many European politicians are demanding more national sovereign control over the application of existing EU laws and the design of new forms of integration.

Few European leaders appear willing to continue relinquishing their countries' sovereignty.

In this context, the hope that the EU might provide a template for liberal regional integration elsewhere seems increasingly lost. The Association of Southeast Asian Nations, South America's Mercosur, the African Union, and the Gulf Cooperation Council remain mechanisms for only limited political and economic cooperation among governments. China and Russia, meanwhile, have used this period of Western self-doubt to modernize their militaries and assert their regional and geopolitical interests. They have built institutions, including the Eurasian Economic Union and the Shanghai Cooperation Organization, that have helped them coordinate and legitimize a parallel political order that challenges Western norms of democratic governance and that rejects any external interference in support of human rights.

AMERICA IN RETREAT

For the past seven decades, the United States has provided the security umbrella under which the liberal international system has flourished. But today, the United States is more inward-looking than at any point since World War II. After the costly wars in Afghanistan and Iraq and the chaos that followed the intervention in Libya, Obama has recalibrated the United States' international role, consistently encouraging allies in Europe and the Middle East to take greater responsibility for their own security. In his presidential campaign, Trump twisted this argument into an explicitly transactional bargain: the United States should become a mercenary superpower, protecting only those countries that pay, so that it can focus on making itself great again at home. In so doing, he ignored the hard-won lesson that investing in the security of U.S. allies is the best way to protect the United States' own security and economic interests. How exactly Trump will govern, however, remains unclear.

Rightly or wrongly, the United States' allies, from Europe to Asia, now fear that the superpower may no longer be an engaged and committed partner. These fears come at a dangerous time. A Europe hobbled by institutional and economic weakness is more vulnerable to the diverse forms of pressure that Russia is currently applying, including financial support for European populist parties and threatening military maneuvers on NATO's eastern borders. Despite Russia's own economic weakness, Putin's advocacy of a new European order based on cultural and national sovereignty appeals to Europe's increasingly vocal nationalist parties, from the UK Independence Party to France's National Front and Hungary's Fidesz, whose leader, Hungarian Prime Minister Viktor Orban, has publicly advocated building an "illiberal state."

NEIL HALL / REUTERS

After the announcement of the result of the United Kingdom's EU referendum, London, June 2016.

Many of the United States' other allies and democratic partners around the world are also on the back foot. Japan and South Korea are struggling to manage the twin challenges of aging populations and economies that are overly dependent on exports, and his-torical antagonisms prevent them from presenting a united front to promote liberal democracy in their region. Large emerging-market democracies, such as Brazil, India, Nigeria, and South Africa, have so far failed to overcome entrenched obstacles to sustainable economic growth and social cohesion. And the perception that U.S. global power is waning and that the Washington consensus does not guarantee economic progress has bolstered strongmen in countries as diverse as the Philippines, Thailand, and Turkey, who have undermined the institutional checks and balances that underpin liberal democracy.

POT, KETTLE

Of course, supporters of the liberal international order have long displayed an inconsistent commitment to its principles. The United States and its allies may have generally promoted respect for the rule of law and liberal governance within their borders, but the dominant objective outside them has been to protect Western security and economic interests, even if doing so damaged the credibility of the liberal international system.

The United States has often acted unilaterally or selectively obeyed the rules of the international order it promotes. It invaded Iraq under a contested legal mandate, and the U.S. Congress has refused to ratify the UN Convention on the Law of the Sea, among numerous other multilateral conventions and treaties. And in 2011, the British, French, and U.S. governments stretched their mandate—granted by UN Security Council Resolution 1973, which authorized all necessary measures to protect civilians in Libya—when they helped overthrow Libya's leader, Muammar al-Qaddafi. And various Western governments have condemned Russia and Syrian President Bashar al-Assad for indiscriminately shelling civilians in Syria while simultaneously supporting Saudi Arabia's bloody campaign in Yemen.

The United States' allies, from Europe to Asia, now fear that the superpower may no longer be an engaged and committed partner.

Small wonder, then, that the West's opponents have interpreted calls to enlarge the liberal international order as an excuse to expand Western political power. Putin sounded this theme in October, at the annual conference of the Valdai Discussion Club, when he accused the United States of promoting globalization and security "for itself, for the few, but not for all." It is also unsurprising that the world's principal multilateral institution, the UN Security Council, remains frozen in the same old standoffs, riven by disagreements between China and Russia, on the one hand, and France, the United Kingdom, and the United States, on the other. As a result, liberal attempts to reform the concept of state sovereignty, such as the introduction of the notion of the responsibility to protect and the establishment of the International Criminal Court, have failed to acquire international legitimacy—take, for instance, the ongoing failure to stem the violence in Syria and the announcements in October by the governments of Burundi, Gambia, and South Africa that they will withdraw from the court. Even the Internet, which promised to foster a more liberal international order by empowering individuals instead of governments, is now increasingly dominated by ideological polarization over national firewalls, surveillance methods, and privacy violations.

KEEPING ORDER

Do these challenges herald the end of the liberal international order? Probably not. Established liberal democracies remain resilient. Whatever domestic challenges they may face, from inequality to unemployment, they approach them from a position of strength compared with emerging-market countries, many of which boast high levels of GDP growth but have yet to make the transition from export- and investment-led growth to consumption- and innovation-driven growth. Western democracies are designed to allow the people to vent their frustrations and refresh their political leadership. Their economies operate in a relatively dynamic, transparent, and open manner, which fosters innovation. These qualities allow their political institutions to recover legitimacy and their economies to regain momentum. On the other hand, centrally controlled or illiberal countries, such as China and Russia, have yet to prove that their political systems will survive the economic transitions they are undertaking.

Still, liberal democracies cannot postpone difficult political decisions any longer. They need to fix themselves first if they are to sustain their liberal international order. They must boost productivity as well as wages, increase work-force participation even as new technologies eliminate old jobs, integrate immigrants while managing aging societies, and, in Europe's case, evolve from centrally funded welfare states to more locally governed welfare societies, in which regions, cities, and other municipalities control a greater share of tax income and so can tailor the provision of social services to local needs. Liberal governments can rise to these challenges, whether by investing more in education, improving physical and digital infrastructure, or modernizing regulations that stifle entrepreneurship and growth in the service sector. These may seem like modest steps. But the appeal and, indeed, the survival of a liberal international order depend on its ability to deliver returns to the societies within it that are superior to any alternative.

If the liberal world can get itself back on track, and does not itself turn to protectionism, it will likely find that the non-Western rising powers, China chief among them, will want to sustain the existing international economic order of relatively open markets and free flows of investment. After all, only through continued integration into the global supply chain of goods, services, people, and knowledge can emerging markets meet the aspirations of their growing middle classes. As the scholar G. John Ikenberry noted in his 2011 book, Liberal Leviathan, the United States and China—the two powers that will most likely determine the future of world order—may both refuse to compromise on their core principles of domestic governance and national security, but they can best coexist and prosper within a liberal international economic order.

It is in the West's interests, therefore, that China's economic development continue smoothly. U.S and European markets for goods, services, and infrastructure should remain open to Chinese foreign direct investment, as long as Chinese companies abide by U.S. and European rules on security and transparency and the protection of intellectual property. European countries should take the same approach with Russia, on the condition that Russian companies abide by EU rules. A mutual commitment to the liberal international economic order would help Western governments and their illiberal counterparts keep open other avenues for cooperation on shared challenges, such as terrorism and climate change, much as China and the United States have done over the past several years.

Western democracies are designed to allow the people to vent their frustrations and refresh their political leadership.

Meanwhile, European governments and businesses should take part in the Chinese-led effort to connect Northeast Asia with Europe across the Eurasian continent, a component of a series of regional infrastructure projects known as the Belt and Road Initiative. In 2016, the volume of global trade stagnated for the first quarter and then fell by 0.8 percent in the second. This reflects an ongoing structural decline in the growth rate of trade, as emerging markets, such as China, make more of their own products and developed countries bring some production back onshore. Against this backdrop, ramping up investment in infrastructure that can connect the thriving coastal areas of Asia to its underdeveloped hinterlands and then to Europe could create new opportunities for economic growth in both the liberal and the illiberal worlds. Rather than challenge such initiatives, the United States should support Western-led regional and multilateral financial institutions, such as the World Bank, the European Bank for Reconstruction and Development, and the Asian Development Bank, as they join forces with the Asian Infrastructure Investment Bank and the New Development Bank (set up by the BRICS countries— Brazil, Russia, India, China, and South Africa) to pursue projects that are in every country's economic interest while adhering to environmentally and financially sustainable principles.

Similar cooperation will be harder to build with Russia. Russia's system of centralized and opaque political and economic governance makes deeper integration incompatible with the EU's market and rules-based system, and NATO members have begun a much-needed upgrading of their military readiness in the face of recent Russian provocations. EU and NATO tensions with Russia will likely persist, even if Trump's election heralds a change in U.S.-Russian relations. Still, the Chinese initiative to build new ways of connecting the Eurasian economy could provide an alternative way for the United States and Europe to engage with Russia.

The countries that built the liberal international order are weaker today than they have been for three generations. They no longer serve as an example to others of the strength of liberal systems of economic and political governance. Autocratic governments may therefore try to establish an alternative political order, one governed by might rather than by international laws and rules.

But liberal policymakers would be wrong to urge their countries to hunker down or resort to containment. An extended standoff between supporters of a liberal international order and those who contest it may accidentally lead to outright conflict. A better approach would be for liberal countries to prepare themselves for a period of awkward coexistence with illiberal ones, cooperating on some occasions and competing on others. The international political world will remain divided between liberals and statists for the foreseeable future, but both sets of countries will depend on a liberal international economic order for their prosperity and internal security. Time will tell whose form of government is more resilient. If history is any guide, liberal democracy remains the best bet.

ROBIN NIBLETT is Director of Chatham House.

© Foreign Affairs

The Once and Future Order

What Comes After Hegemony?

Michael J. Mazarr

Crossing the line: Russian soldiers in Crimea, March 2014

Few foreign policy issues have attracted more attention in recent years than the problem of sustaining the U.S.-led liberal international order. After World War II, the United States sponsored a set of institutions, rules, and norms designed to avoid repeating the mistakes of the 1930s and promote peace, prosperity, and democracy. The resulting system has served as the bedrock of U.S. national security strategy ever since. In everything from arms control to peacekeeping to trade to human rights, marrying U.S. power and international norms and institutions has achieved significant results. Washington continues to put maintaining the international order at the center of the United States' global role.

Yet the survival of that order—indeed, of any ordering principles at all—now seems in question. Dissatisfied countries such as China and Russia view its operation as unjust, and people around the world are angry about the economic and social price they've had to pay for globalization.

It's not clear exactly what President-elect Donald Trump's views are on the role of the United States in the world, much less the liberal order, but his administration will confront the most profound foreign policy task that any new administration has faced in 70 years: rethinking the role that the international order should play in U.S. grand strategy. Whatever Trump's own views, the instincts of many in Washington will be to attempt to restore a unified, U.S.-dominated system by confronting the rule breakers and aggressively promoting liberal values. This would be the wrong approach; in trying to hold the old order together, Washington could end up accelerating its dissolution. What the United States must learn to do instead is navigate and lead the more diversified, pluralistic system that is now materializing—one with a bigger role for emerging-market powers and more ways for countries other than the United States to lead than the current order provides.

THE HOUSE THAT WE BUILT

The creation of the current order, like that of its two modern predecessors—the Concert of Europe and the League of Nations—was an effort to design the basic architecture of international relations in the wake of a war among major powers. All three orders used a range of tools—organizations, treaties, informal meetings, and norms—to attain the goals of their creators. The current order's main institutions include the United Nations, NATO, the World Trade Organization, the International Monetary Fund (IMF), the World Bank, and the G-20.

Together, these bodies have influenced almost every aspect of the modern world. The UN has provided a forum for the international community to rally around shared interests and ratify joint action. The international financial institutions have boosted trade and stabilized the global economy during crises. Multilateral treaties and agreements brokered through various bodies have helped avoid chaotic arms races and uncontrolled nuclear proliferation. And dense global networks of experts, activists, businesses, and nonprofits, operating within the framework of the liberal order, have built consensus and taken action on hundreds of other issues.

It's not clear exactly what Trump's views are on the role of the United States in the world.

The rules of any such order are not self-enforcing. When combined with direct state power, however, they encourage governments to accept norms of conduct such as nonaggression, the avoidance of nuclear weapons, and respect for human rights. The United States would be wise to do what it can to sustain these norms in the future. The trick is figuring out how to do so—and what, given all the changes the world is now experiencing, the emerging order should look like.

THE NOT-SO-LIBERAL ORDER

The postwar liberal order has proved remarkably stable. But it has always incorporated two distinct and not necessarily reconcilable visions. One is a narrow, cautious view of the UN and the core international financial institutions as guardians of sovereign equality, territorial inviolability, and a limited degree of free trade. The other is a more ambitious agenda: protecting human rights, fostering democratic political systems, promoting free-market economic reforms, and encouraging good governance.

Until recently, the tension between these two visions did not pose a serious problem. For many decades, the Cold War allowed the United States and its allies to gloss over the gap in the name of upholding a unified front against the Soviets. After the collapse of the Soviet Union, Washington fully embraced the more ambitious approach by expanding NATO up to Russia's doorstep; intervening to protect human rights in places such as the Balkans and Libya; supporting uprisings, at least rhetorically, in the name of democracy in countries including Egypt, Georgia, and Myanmar; and applying increasingly sophisticated economic sanctions to illiberal governments. In the newly unipolar international system, Washington often behaved as if the narrower concept of order had been superseded by the more ambitious one.

At the same time, the United States often took advantage of its preeminence to sidestep the order's rules and institutions when it found them inconvenient. The problem with this approach, of course, is that international orders gain much of their potency by defining the sources of prestige and status within the system, such as participation in and leadership of international institutions. Their stability depends on leading members abiding—and being seen to abide—by key norms of behavior. When the leader of an order consistently appears to others to interpret the rules as it sees fit, the legitimacy of the system is undermined and other countries come to believe that the order offends, rather than sustains, their dignity.

An extreme version of this occurred in the 1930s, when a series of perceived insults convinced Japan—once a strong supporter of the League of Nations—that the system was a racist, Anglo-American cabal designed to emasculate it. Partly as a result, Japan withdrew from the league and signed the Tripartite Pact with Germany and Italy before entering World War II. Today, a similar story is playing out as some countries see the United States as applying norms selectively and in its own favor, norms that are already tailored to U.S. interests. This is persuading them that the system's main function is to validate the United States' status and prestige at the expense of their own.

The United States would be wise to do what it can to sustain the order's achievements.

For years now, a number of countries, including Brazil, India, South Africa, and Turkey, have found various ways to express their frustration with the current rules. But China and Russia have become the two most important dissenters. These two countries view the order very differently and have divergent ambitions and strategies. Yet their broad complaints have much in common. Both countries feel disenfranchised by a U.S.-dominated system that imposes strict conditions on their participation and, they believe, menaces their regimes by promoting democracy. And both countries have called for fundamental reforms to make the order less imperial and more pluralistic.

DAMIR SAGOLJ / REUTERS

Honor guards at the Great Hall of the People in Beijing, July 2014

Russian officials are particularly disillusioned. They believe that they made an honest effort to join Western-led institutions after the fall of the Soviet Union but were spurned by the West, which subjected them to a long series of insults: NATO's attacks on Serbia in the Balkan wars of the 1990s; NATO enlargement into eastern Europe; and Western support for "color revolutions" in the early years of the new century, which threatened or in some cases actually overthrew Russian-backed leaders in several eastern European countries. In a June 2016 speech to Russian diplomats, Russian President Vladimir Putin complained that certain Western states "continue stubborn attempts to retain their monopoly on geopolitical domination," arguing that this was leading to a "confrontation between different visions of how to build the global governance mechanisms in the 21st century." And Putin hasn't just limited himself to complaining. In recent years, Russia has taken a number of dramatic, sometimes violent steps—especially in Europe—to weaken the U.S.-led order.

China also feels disrespected. The financial crisis at the end of the last decade convinced many Chinese that the West had entered a period of rapid decline and that China deserved a more powerful voice in the international system. Since then, Beijing has increased its influence in several institutions, including the IMF and the World Bank. But the changes have not gone far enough for many Chinese leaders. They still chafe at Western domination of these bodies, perceive U.S. democracy promotion as a threat, and resent the regional network of U.S. alliances that surrounds China. Beijing has thus undertaken a range of economic initiatives to gain more influence within the current order, including increasing its development aid and founding the Asian Infrastructure Investment Bank, which it clearly intends to compete with the IMF and the World Bank. China has also pursued its interests in defiance of global norms by building islands in contested international waters and harassing U.S. aircraft in the South China Sea.

Worrisome as these developments are, it is important not to exaggerate the threats they represent. Neither China nor Russia has declared itself an enemy of the postwar order (although Russia is certainly moving in that direction). Both continue to praise the core UN system and participate actively in a host of institutions, treaties, and diplomatic processes. Indeed, China has worked hard to embed itself ever more firmly in the current order. In a 2015 speech in Seattle, Chinese President Xi Jinping said that "China has been a participant, builder, and contributor" in, of, and to the system and that it stood "firmly for the international order" based on the purposes and principles outlined in the UN Charter. China and Russia both rely on cross-border trade, international energy markets, and global information networks—all of which depend heavily on international rules and institutions. And at least for the time being, neither country seems anxious to challenge the order militarily.

The United States often took advantage of its preeminence to sidestep the order's rules.

Many major countries, including China and Russia, are groping toward roles appropriate to their growing power in a rapidly evolving international system. If that system is going to persevere, their grievances and ambitions must be accommodated. This will require a more flexible, pluralistic approach to institutions, rules, and norms.

ALL THE RAGE

Another threat to the liberal order comes from the populist uprisings now under way in many countries around the world, which have been spurred on by outrage at increasing economic inequality, uneasiness with cultural and demographic changes, and anger at a perceived loss of national sovereignty. For the liberal order to survive, the populations of its member countries must embrace its basic social and political values. That embrace is now weakening.

The postwar order has driven global integration and liberalization by encouraging free-trade agreements, developing international law, and fostering global communications networks. Such developments strengthened the order in turn by cementing public support for liberal values. But the populist rebellion against globalization now imperils that virtuous circle.

The populist surge has featured outbursts in Europe and the United States against the perceived intrusions of a globalizing order. Public support for new trade agreements has tumbled. Resentment toward supranational authorities, such as the European Union, has risen steadily, as has suspicion of and hostility toward immigrants and immigration. The uprising has already claimed one major casualty—the United Kingdom's EU membership—and is mutating into angry, xenophobic nationalism in countries as diverse as Austria, Denmark, France, Greece, Hungary, the Netherlands, Russia, Sweden, and the United States.

Trump and Nigel Farage at a campaign rally in Jackson, Mississippi, August 2016

So far, none of these countries has totally rejected the international order. Populism remains a minority trend in most electorates, and support for liberal principles remains robust in many countries. In a 2016 Gallup survey, for example, 58 percent of Americans polled indicated that they saw trade as an opportunity rather than a threat—the highest number since 1992. Similarly, a 2016 poll by the Pew Research Center found that support for the UN among Americans had grown by nine points since 2004, to a new peak of 64 percent.

Reassuring as such findings are, however, if even a quarter or a third of citizens turn decisively against liberal values in a critical mass of nations, it can destabilize the entire system. In some cases, this happens because radical parties or individuals can come to power without ever achieving more than a plurality of support. More commonly, a rejectionist bloc can cripple legislatures by obstructing steps, such as trade deals and arms treaties, that would strengthen the prevailing order. And sometimes, as happened with the British vote to leave the EU, committed opponents of the order are joined by a larger number of worried citizens in a successful effort to roll back elements of the system.

MIX IT UP

International orders tend to rest on two pillars: the balance of power and prestige among the leading members and some degree of shared values. Both of these pillars look shaky today. For many years, U.S. grand strategy has been based on the idea that the unitary U.S.-led order reflected universal values, was easy to join, and exercised a gravitational pull on other countries. Those assumptions do not hold as strongly as they once did. If Washington hopes to sustain an international system that can help avoid conflict, raise prosperity, and promote liberal values, it will have to embrace a more diverse order—one that operates in different ways for different countries and regions and on different issues.

The United States will be tempted to resist such a change and to double down on the existing liberal order by following the Cold War playbook: rallying democracies and punishing norm breakers. But such a narrow order would create more embittered outcasts and thus imperil the most fundamental objective of any global order: keeping the peace among great powers. Dividing the world into defenders and opponents of a shared order is also likely to be less feasible than in the past. China's role in the global economy and its standing as a regional power mean that it cannot be isolated in the way the Soviet Union was. Many of today's rising powers, moreover, have preferences that are too diverse to gather into either a U.S.-led system or a bloc opposed to it.

Should China or Russia adopt a significantly more aggressive stance, the United States may find it necessary to focus primarily on containing it and hunker down into a narrow, U.S.-led liberal order. But doing so should remain a last resort. During the Cold War, the central challenge of world politics was to contain—and eventually transform—a single power opposed to the main world order. Today the aim is very different: to prevent war and encourage cooperation among a fractious group of countries. An order that is inclusive and shared will meet that challenge better than one that is narrow, aggressive, and dominated by Washington.

The United States would therefore be better off trying to develop several different yet overlapping forms of order: universal and major-power-centric, global and regional, political and economic, liberal and realist. Washington already does this, to an extent. But the tendency in U.S. strategy, especially since the end of the Cold War, has been to pursue a homogeneous liberal order that all states must join in roughly the same way and that pushes its liberal values on every front. The United States would gain more traction if it consciously embraced a more mixed order and accepted some of the difficult compromises that came with it.

The first element of such a mixed order would be a forum for regular dialogue among the system's leading members. At a time when rivalries are growing and many leading states are eager to have a larger voice in international institutions, the world needs a better way to coordinate interests among the system's major powers—not just China and Russia but also Brazil, France, Germany, India, Indonesia, and Japan, among others. A more inclusive UN Security Council combined with the G-20 and various regional and informal conferences would help find areas where major powers can cooperate and smooth over differences among them. This part of the new order would primarily focus on securing the goals laid down in the UN Charter, especially its prohibition on territorial aggression. It would also concentrate on areas where major-power interests overlap, such as fighting climate change, terrorism, and infectious diseases.

A second element of a new mixed order would focus on economic cooperation by relying on the set of international institutions, including the IMF and the World Bank, that have proved so effective at stabilizing the global economy and dealing with financial crises. To ensure that those bodies remain effective, the United States should support enlarging the voting rights of emerging-market powers and work to knit existing institutions together with new ones, such as the Asian Infrastructure Investment Bank. Doing so will be tricky, since it will involve making accommodations to enfranchise non-Western powers while upholding the essential rules of an open trading system.

Reaffirming the economic institutions of the order will be complicated by increasing disagreement over how to achieve economic growth. A number of countries are offering forms of state capitalism as alternatives to the free-market consensus of the postwar order—most notably China, whose government has adopted loose environmental and labor standards and directly supported several industries to give them an advantage over their international competitors. Even within the West, policymakers are divided over the causes of the current economic stagnation. The risk is that if no one can agree on the nature of the problem, nothing will get done. The global economic institutions will have to find ways for the world to nevertheless take joint action, as they did despite similar disagreement when they helped limit the damage of the 2008 financial crisis.

A third part of a mixed order would involve the United States continuing to work with its allies and partners to sustain regional stability and deter aggression. The

United States' role may be less predominant than in the past, but the country is likely to remain an essential spur for joint efforts and a backstop for regional balances of power.

Populism remains a minority trend in most electorates.

Washington will have to calibrate its military posture to defend the order's rules without wrecking relations with other great powers. Assuming that China will continue to ramp up the pressure on the United States and its allies, that Russia will keep pressing its advantages in eastern Europe, and that North Korea will regularly provoke the world with tests of missiles and nuclear weapons, the United States will probably have to expand, rather than shrink, its global military footprint in the coming years. Yet Beijing and Moscow see additional U.S. military deployments in their neighborhoods as threats, so the fundamental challenge for U.S. defense policy in a mixed order will be to bolster deterrence without exacerbating such fears and sparking escalation. Promising ways to do so include establishing advisory programs to increase the military power of regional allies without massive U.S. troop deployments; relying on inherently defensive ways of thinking about operations rather than aggressive, escalatory ones; compromising on provocative deployments, such as missile defenses in eastern Europe; and creating new ways to manage crises when they do occur.

Fourth, the United States would continue to work—sometimes alone, but often with allies—to promote liberal values and systems around the world, but do so in ways that manage, rather than exacerbate, the tensions of a mixed order. This will mean scaling back the more blunt and intrusive methods, such as intervening militarily in defense of human rights or backing opposition democratic movements in countries important to other great powers. But there are plenty of ways to underwrite liberal values without generating blowback. The United States could support ongoing democratic transitions in nations such as Tunisia, for example, or assist established but vulnerable democracies not adjacent to other great powers, such as Colombia or Morocco.

More fundamentally, the United States should increasingly place more indirect and long-term approaches, such as encouraging human development, at the heart of its liberal agenda. This can be done under the auspices of the UN Development Program, which espouses key liberal norms, such as human rights and gender equality, but enjoys broad legitimacy thanks to its UN affiliation and its emphasis on long-term investment over short-term democratic activism. Working through such a structure to create fellowships for young leaders in developing countries and transitioning democracies, training officials in key aspects of good governance, and supporting public health initiatives would be a tremendous investment in the liberal values at the center of U.S. grand strategy without creating the perception that the United States was overreaching.

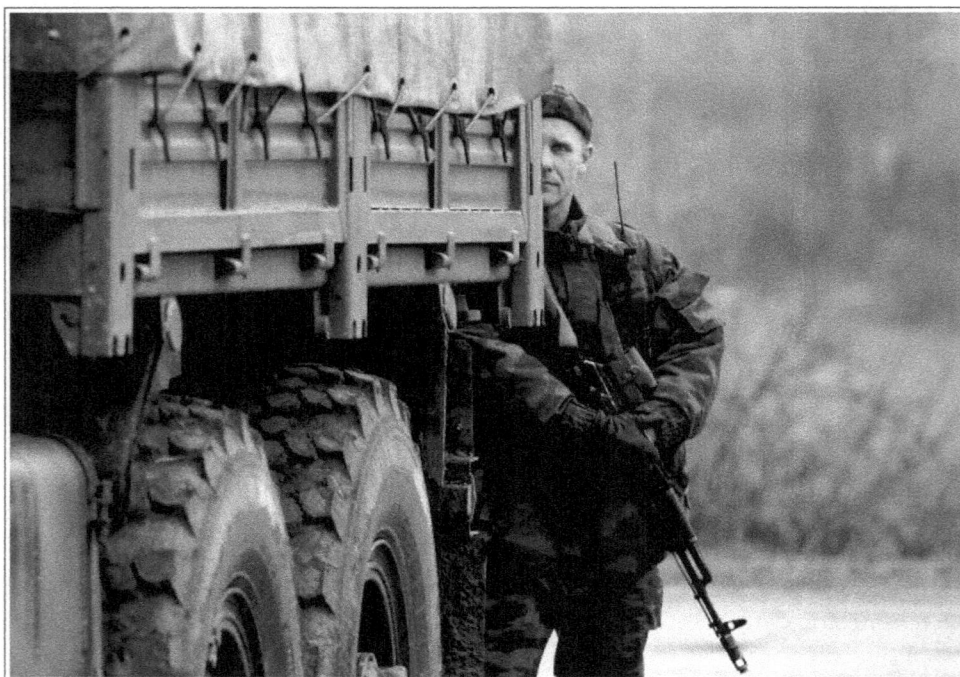

A uniformed man, believed to be a Russian serviceman, outside Sevastopol, March 2014

GIVE-AND-TAKE

In order to manage the contradictions among the various parts of a new mixed order, the United States will have to accept some uncomfortable compromises. There will be constant tension between great-power ties and the promotion of liberal values and between regional and global economic and political rules. Managing these tensions will be the toughest task for U.S. national security strategy over the next decade.

The United States has two ways to approach the problem. One is to identify win-win ideas—areas of cooperation that needn't involve conflicts of values or priorities. There are many issues on which Washington could find such common ground: by working to stabilize financial markets or combat terrorism and infectious diseases, for example.

A second strategy for maintaining balance in a mixed order is to resolve, or at least defer, conflicts that arise out of major powers' claims to spheres of influence. Because of the vital interests involved and the risk of escalation, these pose the greatest threat to global stability. The United States cannot impose its will to resolve these disputes, but if it allows other states to get away with aggression or human rights violations, the whole system could unravel. The biggest mistake of the 1930s, after all, was not liberal overreach but insufficient deterrence of the League of Nation's challengers, Germany and Japan.

This strategy could be employed in the current sovereignty disputes in the South China Sea, for example. The United States could lead a renewed diplomatic effort to defer the issue without jeopardizing any country's claims by getting all the parties to agree to principles over access to resources and maritime movement for a limited time frame and, at the same time, reaffirming shared norms such as nonaggression and the basic principles of maritime law. Getting all sides to agree to this kind of temporary fix would be extremely difficult, but it would still be easier than reaching a final resolution and might ease tensions for a decade or more, thus keeping major-power rivalries from sabotaging the rest of the order.

On these and other issues, the United States cannot abandon its role as the international order's chief sponsor. Although it will no longer be a hegemon presiding over a unified system, it will still be a crucial actor—a catalyst for solutions and a managing partner of a mixed order, each of whose members sees itself as the equal of the others. As influential as rising powers may be, none is prepared to provide decisive direction on any issue. U.S. leadership will remain critical to global stability.

The results will be halting and, very often, unsatisfying. U.S. strategists will have to fashion clear long-term goals, find unifying themes, and explain to the American people the wisdom of diversification and compromise in a more pluralistic world that has become suspicious of grand U.S. projects. For the United States to champion a complex order and step back from liberal overreach would not be a sign of weakness, however. It would simply be an acceptance of the reality of a new, multipolar era, full of restless major powers and roiled by populist rage. The U.S. role in this changing environment will still be to lead the world toward greater peace, prosperity, and respect for liberal values, but in a different way. Getting it right will require an extraordinary balancing act.

MICHAEL J. MAZARR is a Senior Political Scientist at the RAND Corporation and Associate Director of the Strategy, Doctrine, and Resources Program at the RAND Corporation's Arroyo Center.

Global Trumpism

Why Trump's Victory Was 30 Years in the Making and Why It Won't Stop Here

Mark Blyth

Nigel Farage at Trump Tower, New York, November 2016.

Trump's victory was predictable, and was predicted, but not by looking at polls. Polling has taken a beating recently having failed to predict the victory of David Cameron's Conservative Party in the British general elections, then Brexit, and now the election of Donald Trump. One can argue about what's wrong with the methods involved, but more fundamentally what polls do is to treat these phenomena as isolated events when they are in fact the product of a common set of causes 30 years in the making.

There are two issues at play here. The first is known as Galton's problem, after Sir Francis Galton, the inventor of much of modern statistics. Galton's problem is that when we treat cases as independent—the British election, Brexit, the U.S. election— they may not actually be independent. There may be links between the cases—think of Brexit's Nigel Farage showing up at Trump's rallies—and there could be subtler contagion or mimicry effects in play as information from one case "infects" the other, changing the dynamics of the system as a whole. Could there then be a higher set of drivers in the global economy pushing the world in a direction where Trump is really just one part of a more global pattern of events?

Consider that there are many Trumpets blowing around the developed world, on both the right and the left. On the one side, insurgent right-wing parties are bulldozing the vote shares of traditional centrist parties all over Europe. For example, the Finns Party is the second-largest party in the Finnish parliament. In Sweden, the Swedish Democrats are the third-largest party in parliament. In Hungary, Prime Minister Viktor Orban's political party, Fidesz, runs the country having won two elections. Meanwhile in France, the most popular political party is the National Front, which in all scenarios but one—whatever such exercises are actually worth—is expected to win the first round of voting in the 2017 French presidential election. But when all the other parties in France close ranks to prevent the National Front from winning the second round, it's hardly a victory for democracy. And even in that bulwark of stability, Germany, the upstart Alternative for Germany beat German Chancellor Angela Merkel's Christian Democratic Union into second place in her own backyard.

JOHN KOLESIDIS / REUTERS

A clash outside the Labor Ministry in Athens, Greece, January 2013.

But there is also a left-wing version of this phenomenon. Consider the Scottish National Party (the clue is in the name), which has annihilated every other political party in Scotland, or Podemos in Spain, which has won 69 out of 350 seats in the Spanish parliament. Left-wing upstart Syriza runs Greece—even if it's under Troika tutelage—and Die Linke in Germany is yet another drain on the vote share of the once-dominant Social Democrats, whose own vote share has utterly collapsed.

These parties of course have very different policy stances. The new right favors nationals over immigrants and has, at best, a rather casual relationship with the liberal understanding of human rights. The new left, in contrast, favors redistribution from top to bottom and inclusive rather than exclusionary growth policies. But they also have more in common than we think. They are all pro-welfare (for some people, at least), anti-globalization, and most interestingly, pro-state, and although they say it sotto voce on the right, anti-finance. To see why, consider our second issue.

At the end of World War II, the United States and its allies decided that sustained mass unemployment was an existential threat to capitalism and had to be avoided at all costs. In response, governments everywhere targeted full employment as the master policy variable—trying to get to, and sustain, an unemployment rate of roughly four percent. The problem with doing so, over time, is that targeting any variable long enough undermines the value of the variable itself—a phenomenon known as Goodhart's law.

Long before Goodhart, an economist named Michal Kalecki had already worked this out. Back in 1943, he argued that once you target and sustain full employment over time, it basically becomes costless for labor to move from job to job. Wages in such a world will have to continually rise to hold onto labor, and the only way business can accommodate that is to push up prices. This mechanism, cost-push inflation, where wages and prices chase each other up, emerged in the 1970s and coincided with the end of the Bretton Woods regime and the subsequent oil shocks to produce high inflation in the rich countries of the West in the 1970s. In short, the system undermined itself, as both Goodhart and Kalecki predicted. As countries tried harder and harder to target full employment, the more inflation shot up while profits fell. The 1970s became a kind of "debtor's paradise." As inflation rose, debts fell in real terms, and labor's share of national income rose to an all-time high, while corporate profits remained low and were pummeled by inflation. Unions were powerful and inequality plummeted.

The era of neoliberalism is over. The era of neonationalism has just begun.

But if it was a great time to be a debtor, it was a lousy time to be a creditor. Inflation acts as a tax on the returns on investment and lending. Unsurprisingly in response, employers and creditors mobilized and funded a market-friendly revolution where the goal of full employment was jettisoned for a new target—price stability, aka inflation—to restore the value of debt and discipline labor through unemployment. And it worked. The new order was called neoliberalism.

Over the next thirty years the world was transformed from a debtor's paradise into a creditor's paradise where capital's share of national income rose to an all-time high as labor's share fell as wages stagnated. Productivity rose, but the returns all went to capital. Unions were crushed while labor's ability to push up wages collapsed due to the twin shocks of restrictive legislation and the globalization of production. Parliaments in turn were reduced to tweet-generating talking shops as central banks and policy technocrats wrested control of the economy away from those elected to govern.

But Goodhart's law never went away. Just as targeting full employment undermined itself, so did making inflation the policy target.

Consider that since the 2008 crisis the world's major central banks have dumped at least $12 trillion dollars into the global economy and there is barely any inflation anywhere. Almost a quarter of all European bonds now have negative yields. Unsurprisingly, interest rates are on the floor, and if it were not for the massive purchasing of assets in the Eurozone by the European Central Bank, deflation would be systemic. In sum, we may have created a world in which deflation, not inflation, is the new normal, and that has serious political consequences, which brings us back to Trump.

ALVIN BAEZ / REUTERS

Using an ATM during a power outage in San Juan, Puerto Rico, September 2016.

In a world of disinflation, credit became very cheap and the private sector levered up—massively—with post-crisis household debt now standing at $12.25 trillion in the United States. This is a common story. Wage earners now have too much debt in an environment where wages cannot rise fast enough to reduce those debts. Meanwhile, in a deflation, the opposite of what happens in an inflation occurs. The value of debt increases while the ability to pay off those debts decreases.

Seen this way, what we see is a reversal of power between creditors and debtors as the anti-inflationary regime of the past 30 years undermines itself—what we might call "Goodhart's revenge." In this world, yields compress and creditors fret about their earnings, demanding repayment of debt at all costs. Macro-economically, this makes the situation worse: the debtors can't pay—but politically, and this is crucial—it empowers debtors since they can't pay, won't pay, and still have the right to vote.

The traditional parties of the center-left and center-right, the builders of this anti-inflationary order, get clobbered in such a world, since they are correctly identified by these debtors as the political backers of those demanding repayment in an already unequal system, and all from those with the least assets. This produces anti-creditor, pro-debtor coalitions-in-waiting that are ripe for the picking by insurgents of the left and the right, which is exactly what has happened.

In short, to understand the election of Donald Trump we need to listen to the trumpets blowing everywhere in the highly indebted developed countries and the people who vote for them.

The global revolt against elites is not just driven by revulsion and loss and racism. It's also driven by the global economy itself. This is a global phenomenon that marks one thing above all. The era of neoliberalism is over. The era of neonationalism has just begun.

Mark Blyth is Eastman Professor of Political Economy at Brown University.

Trump and World Order

The Return of Self-Help

Stewart M. Patrick

A friend in need: U.S. soldiers in Zagan, Poland, January 2017.

Since the administration of Franklin Roosevelt, 13 successive U.S. presidents have agreed that the United States must assume the mantle of global leadership. Although foreign policy varied from president to president, all sent the clear message that the country stood for more than just its own well-being and that the world economy was not a zero-sum game.

That is about to change. U.S. President Donald Trump has promised a foreign policy that is nationalist and transactional, focused on securing narrow material gains for the United States. He has enunciated no broader vision of the United States' traditional role as defender of the free world, much less outlined how the country might play that part. In foreign policy and economics, he has made clear that the pursuit of narrow national advantage will guide his policies—apparently regardless of the impact on the liberal world order that the United States has championed since 1945.

That order was fraying well before November 8. It had been battered from without by challenges from China and Russia and weakened from within by economic malaise in Japan and crises in Europe, including the epochal Brexit vote last year. No one knows what Trump will do as president. But as a candidate, he vowed to shake up world politics by reassessing long-standing U.S. alliances, ripping up existing U.S. trade deals, raising trade barriers against China, disavowing the Paris climate agreement, and repudiating the nuclear accord with Iran. Should he follow through on these provocative plans, Trump will unleash forces beyond his control, sharpening the crisis of the Western-centered order.

Some countries will resist this new course, joining alliances intended to oppose U.S. influence or thwarting U.S. aims within international institutions. Others will simply acquiesce, trying to maintain ties with Washington because they feel they have no other options, wish to retain certain security and economic benefits, or share a sense of ideological kinship. Still others will react to a suddenly unpredictable United States by starting to hedge their bets.

Hedging is most common when great powers are unpredictable and the global distribution of power is shifting fast—in other words, during times like today.

Like investors, states can manage their risk by diversifying their portfolios. Just as financiers cope with market volatility by making side bets, so countries reduce their vulnerability to unpredictable great powers by sending mixed signals about their alignment. Confronting two great powers, the hedger declines to side with either one, trying to get along with both, placing parallel bets in the hopes of avoiding both domination and abandonment. Hedging is most common when great powers are unpredictable and the global distribution of power is shifting fast—in other words, during times like today.

In recent years, hedging has been confined to Asia, where several of China's neighbors have responded to its rise by welcoming a U.S. security presence in the region but have stopped short of signing treaties to become full-fledged U.S. allies. Indonesia, Myanmar, Singapore, and Vietnam have all adopted a variant of this strategy. But given the uncertainty about U.S. leadership in the age of Trump, hedging could now spread far beyond Asia.

If this scenario plays out, what would be signs that traditional U.S. partners have begun to hedge their bets? Put differently, what are the canaries in the coal mines around the world that would signal an eroding world order? The warning signs look different in three categories of international relations: geopolitics, economics, and climate change. But in all, they would signal a dwindling faith in the post-1945 liberal order and its longtime champion.

A Vietnamese soldier standing guard at Thuyen Chai Island in the Spratly Islands, January 2013.

INSECURITY SYSTEM

Hedging would prove most dramatic in geopolitics. Since 1945, the United States has acted as the ultimate guarantor of world order and of regional power balances. Its forward-leaning military presence, nuclear umbrella, and defense guarantees have provided security for many countries that would otherwise have to fend for themselves in an anarchic global system. Trump may abandon all that. Before and after his election, he made provocative statements that caused foreigners to mistrust their long-standing assumptions about U.S. intentions. He called into question the reliability of U.S. alliance commitments and toyed with the prospect of encouraging U.S. allies, such as Japan, to get their own nuclear arsenals.

Think of the United States as an insurance agency. What would happen if Trump canceled its insurance policies, dramatically increased individual premiums, or cast doubt on payouts? In all likelihood, some policyholders would begin hedging their bets between the United States and the most relevant regional power—China in

Asia, Russia in Europe, and Iran in the Middle East. Such hedging would partly take place internally, as countries built up their individual capabilities for self-defense and bolstered regional bodies. But it would also occur externally, as traditional U.S. partners accommodated U.S. rivals and made their own ultimate intentions unclear.

Hedging would serve as an important signaling device. By increasing the ambiguity of their alignment, states could demonstrate to Washington that it is not the only party capable of pursuing strategic flexibility and imposing costs on former partners. Hedging would also suggest to the aspiring regional hegemon that new opportunities for cooperation were available, provided that certain limits were observed. Current U.S. partners would in effect be trading alignment with Washington—a diminishing asset given Trump's unpredictability—for greater autonomy.

In Asia, hedging against U.S. unreliability could upend the regional security order. Although China now stands at the center of the Asian economy, the United States has, since World War II, guaranteed security through a network of alliances and partnerships. But this could change if the Trump administration increases uncertainty about Washington's staying power in the region by reversing the Obama administration's "pivot" to Asia, withholding U.S. security guarantees unless allies pay more for their own defense, or advocating nuclear proliferation in the region.

If U.S. partners in Asia decided to hedge, the signs would be obvious. Some of them might invest more in independent military capabilities, with Japan and South Korea, in particular, perhaps seriously considering starting nuclear weapons programs. States might seek to create some sort of regional security organization in which both the United States and China would be members but in which neither would dominate. They might make accommodating statements regarding Chinese maritime claims in the East China and South China Seas and publicly criticize U.S. military deployments. They might attempt to bolster the Association of Southeast Asian Nations' limited security role, and Japan, South Korea, India, and Australia might enhance their security cooperation without involving the United States. Vietnam could undertake a gradual rapprochement with China. Erstwhile U.S. partners, such as Singapore, might even start buying weapons from China and training with its forces. Japan and South Korea might enhance their trilateral strategic dialogue with China on North Korea and other issues. Meanwhile, the momentum behind U.S partnerships with India, Indonesia, and Vietnam might slow, and Asian states could increasingly resort to ad hoc coalitions of their own to deal with specific regional security problems.

What are the canaries in the coal mines around the world that would signal an eroding world order?

In Europe, U.S. allies would hedge in response to weaker transatlantic ties, eroding U.S. commitments to NATO, or the prospect of a Washington-Moscow condominium that would transform European states into pawns. The continent's big four—France, Germany, Italy, and the United Kingdom—would likely increase their defense spending and security cooperation, perhaps including Belgium, Luxembourg, and the Netherlands, too. Some European leaders would start employing Gaullist language, depicting the continent (and perhaps the EU as a body) as a natural balancer between the United States and Russia. Eastern European states could respond to growing vulnerability—and the declining credibility of NATO—by accommodating Russia, rearming their militaries, and reinvigorating the EU's Common Security and Defense Policy. The suddenly vulnerable Baltic states could turn away from the United States and submit to "Finlandization," a more neutral stance that would allow Moscow greater control over their policies. Ukraine, meanwhile, would likely adopt a more conciliatory policy toward Russia, perhaps flirting with membership in the Eurasian Economic Union or with acceptance of its own de facto partition. Turkey, an increasingly tenuous NATO member, would likely try to curry favor with both Russia and the United States, playing off each against the other.

Security hedging in the Middle East would accentuate trends visible during the Obama administration, including waning U.S. influence, an increased Russian presence, and growing rivalry between Iran and Sunni powers (notably Saudi Arabia). Even Israel, whose right-wing government Trump has embraced, would tighten links with Russia as a hedge against U.S. retrenchment. Out of a fear that the United States would prove less willing to check Iran, the members of the Gulf Cooperation Council (Bahrain, Kuwait, Oman, Qatar, Saudi Arabia, and the United Arab Emirates) would ramp up their defense spending, enhance their cooperation, and undertake discrete negotiations with Tehran aimed at limiting its worst behavior.

Hedging is less likely in the Americas, given the scale of U.S. dominance. That said, the region's countries could begin to elevate the Community of Latin American and Caribbean States, which excludes the United States and Canada, above the Organization of American States, which includes them. In sub-Saharan Africa, lastly, little geopolitical hedging should take place, since the region remains a marginal setting for great-power competition, relatively speaking.

John Kerry, then the U.S. secretary of state, speaks with members of the U.S. delegation after a meeting with Iranian officials in Lausanne, Switzerland, Mach 2015.

THE RETURN OF MERCANTILISM

Economic hedging is inherently different from its geopolitical counterpart. After all, global trade and investment hold the promise of absolute gains for all, and national survival is not immediately at stake. Still, given Trump's campaign pledges to upend the open, liberal system of trade that the United States has promoted since 1945, traditional U.S. trading partners will surely hedge their bets.

Trump has pledged to tear up "horrible" trade deals, including the North American Free Trade Agreement and the Trans-Pacific Partnership; declare China a currency manipulator; and slap a 45 percent tariff on Chinese imports. If his administration pursues such a mercantilist course, U.S. trading partners will rightly conclude that the United States is abandoning its global economic leadership and support for open markets. Beyond retaliating against U.S. protectionism and seeking remedies within the dispute-settlement mechanism of the World Trade Organization, they could respond to perceived U.S. exploitation in several ways.

Current U.S. trading partners would look to other major economies, particularly China, and blocs, such as the European Union, to become the new motor for the liberalization of global trade. They would likely shift their energies toward alternative arrangements that do not involve the United States—such as the Regional Comprehensive Economic Partnership, the Belt and Road Initiative, and the Asian Infrastructure Investment Bank, all led by China—to secure more promising markets for goods and fields for investment. U.S. trading partners might well diversify their foreign currency reserves away from dollar holdings and conduct more trade in euros, pounds, yen, and yuan. Emerging economies would redouble their efforts to reduce U.S. influence in the International Monetary Fund and the World Bank (and openly resist the informal U.S. prerogative to choose the head of the latter body). And developing countries seeking financing would increasingly look to nontraditional donors, such as Brazil, China, India, and the United Arab Emirates.

If the United States abdicates its global economic leadership, it will leave the world economy adrift at a precarious moment. Without a firm hand at the helm, the G-7 group of advanced market democracies could risk fading into irrelevance. The more inclusive G-20 would look increasingly to Beijing for leadership. The BRICS coalition of Brazil, Russia, India, China, and South Africa could find new purpose, particularly if its three emerging-market democracies perceived China as a better economic partner than the United States.

PLANETARY PERIL

Finally, some countries will hedge against uncertain U.S. leadership when it comes to preserving a sustainable planet. Global warming poses the biggest long-term threat to the survival of the human species. As a candidate, Trump described climate change, which scientists overwhelming accept as real and largely man-made, as a "hoax" perpetrated by the Chinese, and he pledged to shred the 2015 Paris agreement, an ambitious emissions-reduction pact.

If the Trump administration does abrogate that agreement, some parties to it will push back, whereas others will simply consider it dead. Many, however, will hedge. Rather than repudiate the accord outright, they will make their own commitments to it more ambiguous. They might extend the deadlines for their own cuts, shift their focus from mitigating climate change to adapting to it, or simply move it down their list of global priorities.

Some countries will hedge against uncertain U.S. leadership when it comes to preserving a sustainable planet.

Countries that decided to keep climate change a priority might attempt to force Washington to address the issue regardless by inserting emissions targets and other climate commitments into unrelated pacts, such as ones concerning trade or agriculture. To get the United States to assume some of the cost of the environmental externalities created by its defection from the climate change regime, they could levy tariffs on U.S. goods based on how much carbon was emitted during their production. They might also engage directly with environmentally minded U.S. states (such as California) or even municipalities (such as New York City) to reach agreements on emissions reductions.

STEPHANE MAHE / REUTERS

Officials at the final plenary session of the negotiations for the Paris climate agreement, near Paris, France, December 2015.

Unlike in the geopolitical and economic realms, hedging on climate change would prove deeply unsatisfactory for the countries that did it, since although they would be avoiding short-term sacrifices, their actions would increase the risk of planetary catastrophe. And because greenhouse gases have a global effect, countries disappointed or alienated by U.S. behavior would have no alternative system with which to align themselves—no climate equivalent to a Chinese-led security order, for instance.

TRUMP'S CHOICE

A future in which other countries hedge as the United States abandons its decades-long leadership is not preordained. Whether it comes to pass will depend on the choices Trump makes as president. If he pivots away from his campaign pledges—in response to the advice of senior advisers, pressure from Congress, or pleas from foreign leaders—his administration could revert to a more standard U.S. grand strategy. But if he makes life riskier for longtime partners—by weakening U.S. alliance commitments, adopting protectionist economic policies, and shirking obligations to combat global warming—U.S. allies and partners will seek to advance their national security, prosperity, and well-being through increased autonomy. In that case, the Trump administration will find that its attempts to expand the United States' freedom of action and keep others guessing will be met in kind, to the benefit of U.S. rivals and to the detriment of U.S. economic interests and the health of the planet.

That would be an ironic outcome. A leitmotif of Trump's presidential campaign was the need to reduce Americans' vulnerability to international threats and unfair economic competition. And yet the steps Trump has endorsed risk driving away U.S. allies and partners, exposing Americans to global instability and economic retaliation, and accelerating the demise of the world the United States made.

STEWART M. PATRICK is James H. Binger Senior Fellow in Global Governance and Director of the International Institutions and Global Governance Program at the Council on Foreign Relations. Follow him on Twitter @StewartMPatrick.